Plants

Grades 4–6

INVESTIGATING SCIENCE

Project Manager:
Elizabeth H. Lindsay

Writers:
Julie Granchelli, Beth Gress, Dan Kreisberg, Karen P. Scott

Editors:
Cayce Guiliano, Peggy W. Hambright, Deborah T. Kalwat,
Scott Lyons, Jennifer Munnerlyn

Art Coordinator:
Clevell Harris

Artists:
Nick Greenwood, Clevell Harris, Greg D. Rieves,
Barry Slate, Donna K. Teal

Cover Artists:
Nick Greenwood and Kimberly Richard

www.themailbox.com

©2000 by THE EDUCATION CENTER, INC.
All rights reserved.
ISBN #1-56234-401-3

Manufactured in the United States
10 9 8 7 6 5 4 3 2

Table of Contents

Water

About This Book

Welcome to *Investigating Science—Plants*! This book is one of eight must-have resource books that support the National Science Education Standards and are designed to supplement and enhance your existing science curriculum. Packed with practical cross-curricular ideas and thought-provoking reproducibles, these all-new, content-specific resource books provide intermediate teachers with a collection of innovative and fun activities for teaching thematic science units.

Included in this book:

Investigating Science—Plants contains five cross-curricular thematic units, each containing
- Background information for the teacher
- Easy-to-implement instructions for science experiments and projects
- Student-centered activities and reproducibles
- Literature links

Cross-curricular thematic units found in this book:
- *Plants*
- *Four Essentials*
- *Seeds*
- *Life Cycles*
- *Trees*

Other books in the intermediate Investigating Science series:
- *Investigating Science—Animals*
- *Investigating Science—Weather & Climate*
- *Investigating Science—The Earth*
- *Investigating Science—Space*
- *Investigating Science—The Human Body*
- *Investigating Science—Light & Sound*
- *Investigating Science—Energy, Magnetism, & Machines*

Plants

Use the following activities and reproducibles to plant a host of horticultural knowledge in your students' minds!

Background for the Teacher

- *Plants* are living organisms that are rooted in the soil; possess cellulose cell walls; and make their own food from air, sunlight, and water—a process called *photosynthesis*.
- During photosynthesis, *chlorophyll,* a chemical found in green plants, traps energy from the sun. The plant uses this energy to produce its own food.
- Plants are one of the five kingdoms of living things. Botanists separate plants into ten *divisions* according to their overall appearance, their internal structure, and the form of their reproductive organs.
- To date, scientists have classified the more than 300,000 known plant species.
- *Spore-bearing plants*—such as algae, mosses, and ferns—reproduce by releasing many tiny spores, which are then dispersed by the wind or water.
- *Seed-bearing plants* release seeds that hold tiny embryos, which contain all the necessary parts to form the plant as well as a food supply.
- Plants are an important food source. Today, rice, corn, and wheat crops feed more than half of the earth's population.
- Plants such as cotton and flax are used to make clothing.
- Some plants, such as aloe vera, are used in medicines and to treat skin wounds.
- Other plants are used to make paper products or are turned into lumber for houses and other structures.
- Most important, plants provide oxygen for humans and animals to breathe.

Clear Classification
(Research, Making a Life-Sized Chart)

Introduce your students to the plant classification system by having them research the many types of plants. To begin, explain to students that botanists consider plants to be one of the five *kingdoms* (overall groups) of living things. They divide this kingdom into ten *divisions* according to a plant's overall appearance, its internal structure, and how it reproduces. Next, put students into ten groups. Assign each group a division from the chart below. Then provide each group with a sheet of poster board, markers or crayons, and access to encyclopedias, books, and other resource materials. Direct each group to research its division to find out about its plants' external and internal appearance, where they live, and how they reproduce. Instruct the group to add pictures to the poster board of the kinds of plants found in its division. Finally, display each division in an organized chart as shown. Encourage students to refer to the chart throughout their study of the plant kingdom.

Conifers
Most conifers have tall, straight trunks and narrow branches. The leaves on conifers in cooler climates are usually sharply tipped needles; flat, narrow leaves; or tiny scalelike leaves. In warmer climates conifer trees usually have broader, oval-shaped leaves. Because most conifers are evergreens, they keep their foliage all year.

Conifers are part of a group called *gymnosperms.* Gymnosperms are plants that have seeds but no flowers. The seeds develop on the woody scales of cones or inside fleshy cups. Conifers have separate female and male cones. The male cones produce pollen, which is carried on the wind to the open female cones, which carry the sex cells. Then the male cones fall to the ground, and seeds develop inside the female cones. Female cones can stay on a tree for many years.

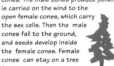

Plant Kingdom

Divisions

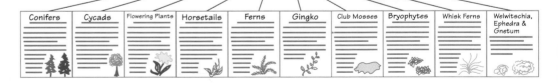

Conifers	Cycads	Flowering Plants	Horsetails	Ferns	Gingko	Club Mosses	Bryophytes	Whisk Ferns	Welwitschia, Ephedra & Gnetum

"Plant-astic" Literature Picks

Flowers (Eyewitness Explorers series) by David Burnie (Dorling Kindersley Publishing, Inc.; 1993)

Janice VanCleave's Plants: Mind-Boggling Experiments You Can Turn Into Science Fair Projects (Spectacular Science Projects series) by Janice VanCleave (John Wiley & Sons, Inc.; 1997)

My Indoor Garden by Carol Lerner (Morrow Junior Books, 1999)

The Nature and Science of Leaves by Jane Burton and Kim Taylor (Gareth Stevens Publishing, 1997)

Venus Flytraps (Early Bird Nature Books series) by Kathleen V. Kudlinski (Lerner Publications Company, 1998)

What's Inside Plants? (What's Inside? series) by Anita Ganeri (Macdonald Young Books, Ltd.; 1993)

Fascinating Flowers
(Making a Model)

Watch your students' observation skills bloom as they learn how to identify the parts of a flower. Begin by making and displaying a transparency of the flower shown. Point out to students the different parts of a flower, and then explain the job or role of each part. Next, provide each student with a copy of page 8, a 9" x 12" sheet of construction paper, markers or crayons, and a copy of the directions below. Have each student follow the directions to make a labeled 3-D flower showing the different parts. Display the flowers on a bulletin board titled "Knowledge in Bloom—Learning the Parts of a Flower."

Figure 1

Figure 2

Figure 3

Figure 4

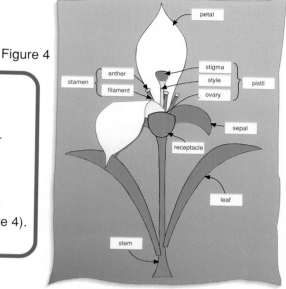

Directions:
1. Color the flower parts on page 8; cut out the flower parts and the words.
2. Glue the stem, both sepals, one petal, and both leaves onto the construction paper (Figure 1).
3. Glue the stamens and the pistil on the petal (Figure 2).
4. Roll the other petal around your pencil (Figure 3).
5. Glue the bottom edge of the petal to the top of the stem so the rolled side faces out. Then glue the receptacle over this petal's base (Figure 4).
6. Label each flower part with the words from page 8.

Wanted: Plants!
(Research, Writing)

Your students will love researching these "wanted" plants as they learn about their amazing and unusual characteristics. Begin by explaining to students that most plants make their food during *photosynthesis* and normally get necessary water and nutrients from the soil. However, some plants have evolved other methods of surviving. These plants are called *parasitic, epiphytic,* or *carnivorous* plants. Parasitic plants attach themselves onto other plants called *hosts.* They steal the hosts' nutrients and mineral supplies. Epiphytic plants also live on hosts, but they do so only to be closer to the sunlight. These plants generally live on a host's branches or stem. Carnivorous plants get their nutrients by capturing small animals and insects in their leaves. They digest these insects by secreting special juices from their leaves, or use bacteria or fungal processes.

Next, pair students; then assign each pair one of the plants from the list below. Direct the pair to use a variety of reference materials to research its plant. Then have each pair make a "wanted" poster on a sheet of white construction paper, using a variety of arts-and-crafts supplies. (See the example shown.) Instruct the pair to include what its plant looks like, how it survives, where it lives, and a detailed picture of the plant. Have the pairs share their "wanted" posters with the class; then combine all the posters into a class book titled "Wanted: Strange and Unusual Plants!"

WANTED!

 Mistletoe

Appearance: seen growing on host's branches

Crime: steals host's water and mineral nutrients

Last known location: found worldwide

Parasitic plants:	Carnivorous plants:	Epiphytic plants:
dodder plant	sundew plant	bromeliad
giant rafflesia	monkey cup pitcher	epiphytic orchid
ghost orchid	marsh pitcher	strangler fig
	yellow trumpet pitcher	epiphylls
	venus flytrap	staghorn fern
	butterwort	
	bladderwort	

"Cell-ebrate" Plants!
(Making a Model, Critical Thinking)

Here's a tasty way to familiarize your students with the structure of a plant cell—constructing edible models! To begin, explain to students that cells can be found in all living things. A plant cell's parts perform specific jobs, are enclosed by a tough *cell wall* that makes them rigid, and contain bright green *organelles* called *chloroplasts.* During *photosynthesis,* chloroplasts convert the sun's energy into food and building materials for the plant. Have each student become more familiar with the parts of a plant cell by giving her a copy of page 9 to complete as directed. Discuss the different parts as a class. Next, place a tub of white spreadable frosting, graham crackers, various decorative frostings, and an assortment of nuts and candies on a table or at a center. Then pair students. In turn, have each pair visit the table and use the supplies and their completed reproducibles to create a model of a plant cell similar to the one shown. Direct the partners to identify each part of their cell and explain why they chose to represent the parts with each chosen food piece. After students have shared their models, allow them to eat their creations.

Further extend this activity by encouraging students to choose one plant cell part; then have the child find an everyday object from home to represent it. For example, a child might choose a battery to represent the *mitochondrion* because mitochondria produce energy in the cell. After each child brings her object to class, have her describe which cell part it represents and why.

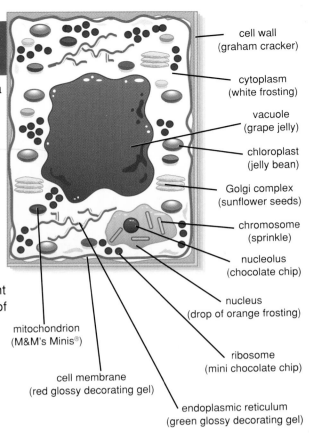

cell wall
(graham cracker)

cytoplasm
(white frosting)

vacuole
(grape jelly)

chloroplast
(jelly bean)

Golgi complex
(sunflower seeds)

chromosome
(sprinkle)

nucleolus
(chocolate chip)

nucleus
(drop of orange frosting)

ribosome
(mini chocolate chip)

mitochondrion
(M&M's Minis®)

endoplasmic reticulum
(green glossy decorating gel)

cell membrane
(red glossy decorating gel)

Botany Record Breakers
(Research, Writing)

Did you know that the largest fruit ever recorded was a 900-pound squash? Have your students discover other interesting facts about record-breaking plants with this research activity. Provide each student with one 9" x 12" sheet each of pink, green, brown, and blue construction paper; one 12" x 18" sheet of yellow construction paper; and markers or crayons. Direct the student to cut out a variety of the following shapes from construction paper: flowers (pink), leaves and a stem (green), roots (blue), and soil (brown). (See diagram on this page.) Then have her glue the cutouts to the yellow paper to create a detailed plant similar to the one shown. Next, have each student use various resource materials to research record-breaking plant statistics. Instruct the student to record one statistic on each of the plant parts as shown. Display the students' plant designs on a bulletin board titled "Botany Record Breakers."

Tallest Plant

Coast redwoods in California can reach 363 feet.

Fastest-Growing Land Plants

Giant bamboo can grow 3 feet each day.

Oldest Plant

Some bristlecone pine trees are thought to be about 4,900 years old.

Smallest Seeds

As many as 2,500 seeds can grow in a single tobacco plant pod that is only ³/₄ inch long.

Largest Seed

Some coconut trees can produce seeds that weigh more than 20 pounds.

Largest Leaves

The raffia palm has leaves that grow up to 65 feet long and 8 feet wide.

Smallest Flowering Plant

The duckweed is only about ¹/₆₀ inch long. It can be found floating on the surface of ponds.

Largest Flowering Plant

Eucalyptus trees can grow more than 300 feet tall.

Hanging Gardens
(Experiment)

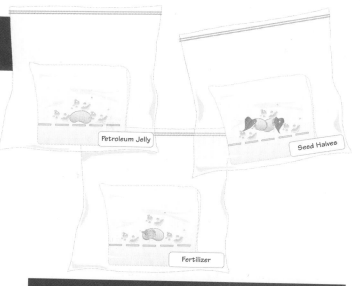

Petroleum Jelly

Seed Halves

Fertilizer

Introduce your students to the world of gardening with this hands-on activity. To begin, divide students into pairs. Designate one pair as the control group; the control group's garden will be the one that is created following the basic directions. Assign each remaining pair a plant test variable from below. Explain to students that they will compare how lima beans grow when certain *variables* are changed. Next, provide each group with a copy of the directions shown and materials from the list below (materials will vary, depending on the variable).

Direct each group to follow the directions, being careful to modify them to fit its variable. Then help the groups tack the top, back edge of their bags along the middle of a sunlit bulletin board, so they can reach the bags. Remind the groups to check their gardens each day, watering them as needed (unless otherwise directed). After seven to ten days, have the groups record their observations and conclusions about how their gardens have grown compared with the control group's garden. *(After several days, each group except A, B, and D should see a root and a stem growing from the bean.)*

Control group: Follow the directions provided to set up the plant bag.

Plant test variables:
  A. Don't water the lima bean.
  B. Water the bean with a vinegar-and-water mixture.
  C. Cover the bag with construction paper to prevent light from reaching the seed.
  D. Do not put wet paper towels in the bag.
  E. Coat the seed with petroleum jelly.
  F. Carefully cut the seed in half; then place both halves in the bag.
  G. Rotate the bag one turn each day.
  H. Add one cup soil to the bag instead of damp paper towels. Do not staple the bag.
  I. Water the bean with a mixture of liquid fertilizer and water.

Materials: quart-sized resealable plastic bags, lima beans, 1 c. soil, paper towels, 3 spritz bottles (1 filled with water, 1 with vinegar and water, 1 with liquid fertilizer and water), construction paper, petroleum jelly, scissors, stapler

Directions:
(Remember to modify these directions to fit your variable.)
  1. Label your bag according to your group.
  2. On a sheet of paper, write a prediction about how you think your garden will grow.
  3. Wet two paper towels; then fold them into a square and place them in the plastic bag.
  4. Staple the paper towels and the bag together about two inches from the bottom of the bag.
  5. Drop the seed into the bag. It should stop at the staples and not reach the bottom of the bag. Seal the bag.

Palatable Plant Parts
(Classifying, Making a Model)

Ask your students if they ate a root or a leaf for dinner last night, and they'll probably think you're crazy! Use the following activity to introduce them to the many edible parts of plants. Explain to students that they probably eat some plant parts—roots, bulbs, stems, leaves, seeds, fruits, and flowers—every day. Provide each student with a copy of page 10 along with markers or crayons, scissors, and glue. Direct the student to complete the reproducible as directed. Next, pair students and provide each pair with a large plastic zippered bag filled with seven food items from the list below. (Be sure to wash the fruits and vegetables thoroughly.) Also give each pair two paper towels and have a stopwatch on hand. Instruct the pair to spread out its food items on one paper towel. Then have the pair position the food on the other paper towel to form a "plant" as shown. Time students as they create their plants. Declare a winner when the fastest pair has correctly positioned each plant part. Finally, allow the pairs to eat their plant, part by part.

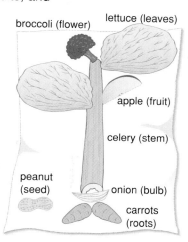

broccoli (flower)
lettuce (leaves)
apple (fruit)
celery (stem)
peanut (seed)
onion (bulb)
carrots (roots)

Edible parts of plants:
Roots: carrots, radishes, sweet potatoes
Bulbs: onions, garlic
Stems: asparagus, green onions, celery
Leaves: cabbage, lettuce, spinach
Flowers: broccoli, cauliflower
Fruits: apples, pears, peaches, cucumbers, pumpkins, tomatoes, peppers
Seeds: peas, beans, corn, peanuts

Pattern

Use with "Fascinating Flowers" on page 5.

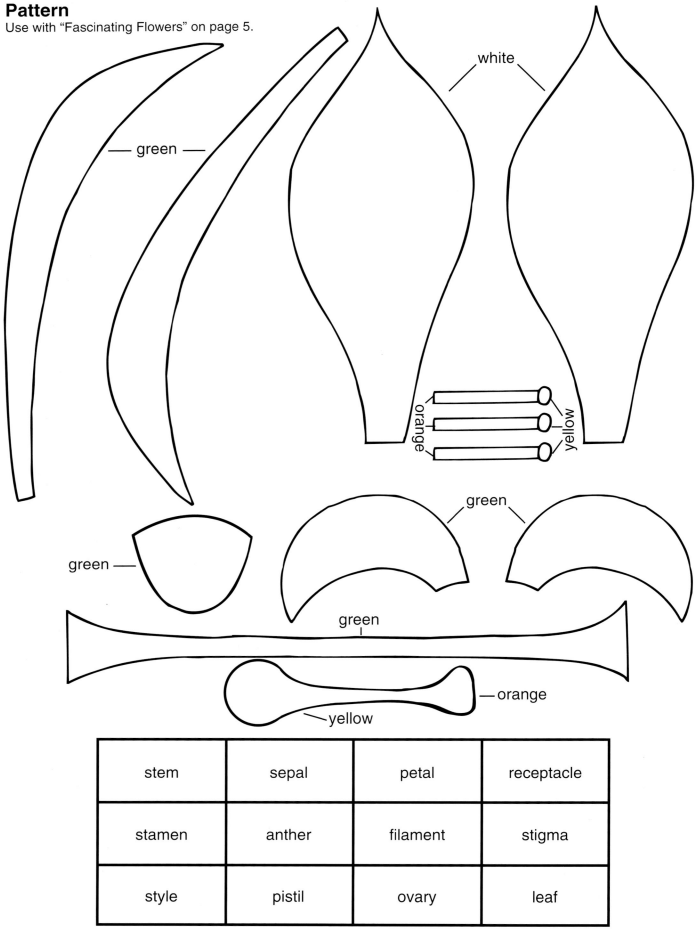

— green —

white

green

orange

yellow

green

green

green

orange

yellow

stem	sepal	petal	receptacle
stamen	anther	filament	stigma
style	pistil	ovary	leaf

Name _____

Cell Structure

Directions: Look at the plant cell diagram below. Read each definition; then write the word that matches the definition on the blank provided. Use an encyclopedia or your textbook to help you.

A sausage-shaped structure that produces the energy the cell needs.

A stack of flat structures that store different products and eventually release them from the cell.

A thin covering that protects the cell and separates it from its surroundings. Controls which materials move into and out of the cell.

The most visible organelle in a plant cell. Controls the activities of the cell.

The most noticeable structure in the *nucleus*. Helps to produce *ribosomes*.

A long, threadlike item that contains DNA, genes, and proteins.

A network of membrane-enclosed channels in the *cytoplasm* that move materials around the cell.

A tiny, round body that helps the cell make its own protein, which helps it grow, repair itself, and perform chemical operations.

A green organelle that contains *chlorophyll* and converts the sun's energy into food for the plant.

A flowing gel-like material that makes up all of the cell but the *nucleus*.

The stiff outer area that surrounds the *cell membrane*.

A large cavity where water and nutrients are stored.

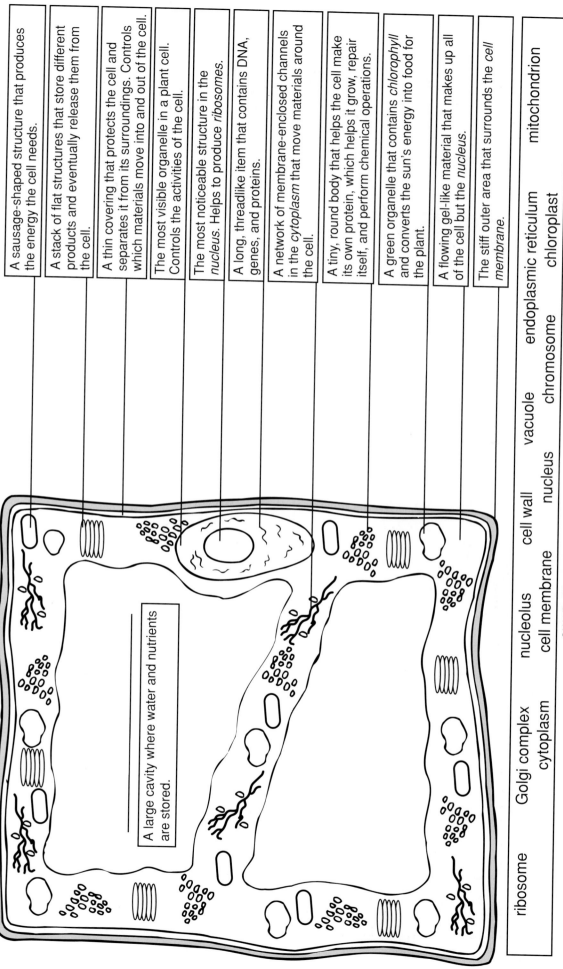

| ribosome | Golgi complex | nucleolus | cell wall | vacuole | endoplasmic reticulum | mitochondrion |
| | cytoplasm | cell membrane | nucleus | chromosome | chloroplast | |

Note to the teacher: Use with "'Cell-ebrate' Plants!" on page 6.

9

Organizing Edibles

You probably didn't realize it, but you eat plant parts all the time! Make an organized chart showing from which part of a plant each common food item comes.

Directions: Color and then cut out the plant part pictures below. Glue each picture on the grid to create an organized chart.

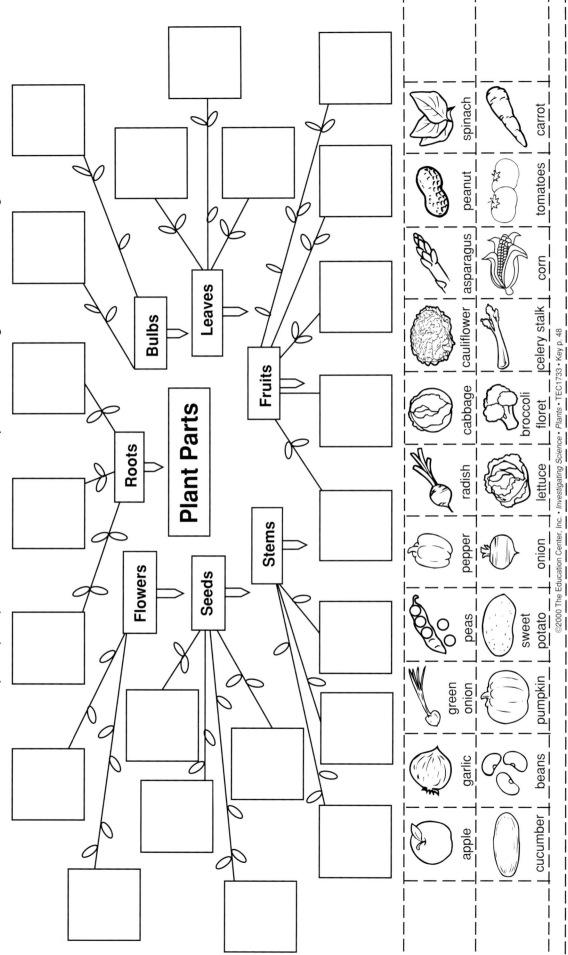

Plant Parts

Roots

Bulbs

Leaves

Flowers

Seeds

Stems

Fruits

spinach	carrot
peanut	tomatoes
asparagus	corn
cauliflower	celery stalk
cabbage	broccoli floret
radish	lettuce
pepper	onion
peas	sweet potato
green onion	pumpkin
garlic	beans
apple	cucumber

©2000 The Education Center, Inc. • *Investigating Science • Plants* • TEC1733 • Key p. 48

Note to the teacher: Use with "Palatable Plant Parts" on page 7.

Name _____

Watch Out!

Did you know that there are about 700 kinds of poisonous plants in the United States and Canada? A poisonous plant is any plant that can injure a person or an animal. Many poisonous plants can be avoided because they look, taste, or smell disagreeable. *(Remember that even some familiar food plants can have poisonous parts!)*

Directions: Read each sentence below. Then use an encyclopedia to help you fill in the spaces with the name of one of the poisonous plants shown. Finally, write the letter for each number in the secret code below.

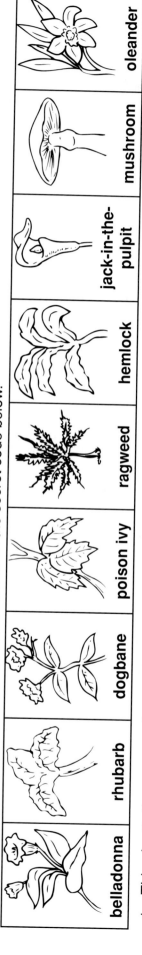

belladonna	rhubarb	dogbane	poison ivy	ragweed	hemlock	jack-in-the-pulpit	mushroom	oleander

1. This plant's tissues contain a poisonous oil that can be irritating to the skin.

   ___ ___ ___ ___ ___ ___ ___ ___ ___
   6   1   7   1   3   5   14 16 5

2. If eaten raw, the needlelike crystals contained on this plant's tissues can injure the mouth and throat.

   ___ ___ ___ ___ ___ ___ ___
   8   11 12   7   13

3. Though it's beautiful, people have died from eating the berries of this plant.

   ___ ___ ___
   6   10 4

4. Many people are allergic to the pollen of this plant.

   ___ ___ ___ ___ ___ ___ ___
   6   4   5   14 16

5. A favorite porch plant in the summer, all parts of this plant are poisonous if eaten.

   ___ ___ ___ ___ ___
   5   9   3   2   1

6. People use this plant's juicy, reddish stalks in desserts. However, the leaves are poisonous.

   ___ ___ ___ ___ ___ ___ ___
   11 12 2   6   4

7. Some of these plants can be fatal if eaten. Those that are poisonous are often called *toadstools.*

   ___ ___ ___ ___ ___ ___ ___ ___
   13 5   14 16 6   5   4

8. All of these green plants are poisonous and contain a bitter milky juice. Luckily, most animals dislike the bitter juice and will not eat this plant.

   ___ ___ ___ ___ ___ ___ ___
   1   2   4   5   3   ,

9. This plant is a poisonous herb that resembles parsley. It can be easily recognized by its foul odor.

   ___ ___ ___ ___ ___ ___ ___ ___ ___ ___ ___
   10 1   12 12 15

©2000 The Education Center, Inc. • *Investigating Science • Plants* • TEC1733 • Key p. 48

Four Essentials

Familiarize students with four fundamental ingredients necessary for healthy plants with this collection of activities, experiments, and reproducibles.

Focusing on Photosynthesis
(Game)

Play this fast-paced game to introduce students to the basic ingredients of *photosynthesis,* the food-making process of green plants. In advance, cut out and label at least four small construction paper squares in the following colors for each child: yellow (sunlight), brown (minerals), gray (carbon dioxide), blue (water). Next, ask students if they could produce food for themselves using only four ingredients—sunlight, water, minerals from the soil, and carbon dioxide from the air. After observing their shocked faces, announce that those ingredients are what *plants* use to make their own food. Briefly explain that *chlorophyll* (green matter) in a plant's leaves traps sunlight, and that together with carbon dioxide from the air and minerals from the water that the roots take in, a plant makes food and oxygen. Then guide students through the steps below to play a game that can help them remember the four key elements of photosynthesis.

Steps:
1. Shuffle the colored squares; then spread them around a large play area.
2. Have each child pretend to be a plant that must make a specific amount of food within an allotted time in order to survive.
3. At your signal, direct students to roam the play area, gathering as many colored squares as they can.
4. When time is up, have each child sort his squares into sets of four squares each: one yellow (sunlight), one brown (minerals), one gray (carbon dioxide), one blue (water).
5. Declare the students collecting at least four complete sets the "survivors."
6. Have each survivor explain to the class why having the sets of four squares makes him a survivor.

Background for the Teacher

Land plants need the right combination of light, water, soil, and air to be healthy.

Light
- Plants need light to grow and make their own food. The food-making process in plants is called *photosynthesis.*
- Different plants require different amounts of light.
- Extremes in heat and cold can affect plant growth.

Water
- Plants need water to grow and make food.
- Different plants require different amounts of water.
- The water absorbed by a plant's roots contains minerals needed for growth.

Soil
- Plants need soil to get magnesium, an important growth mineral, and nutrients such as nitrogen, phosphorus, and potassium.
- Different plants thrive best in particular types of soil.
- *Alkaline* (salty) soil is found in dry, salty deserts. *Acidic* (sour) soil is found in coniferous forests. The best soil is neutral to slightly acidic.

Air
- Plants need carbon dioxide from the air to make food and oxygen. Plants need oxygen to burn food for energy.
- Plants breathe through their leaves and roots.
- Polluted air affects plant growth and can kill a plant.

An "Essen-sational" Literature List

Children's Atlas of the Environment (Rand McNally & Co., 1992)

A Drop of Water: A Book of Science and Wonder by Walter Wick (Scholastic, Inc. 1997)

Earthwatch: Earthcycles and Ecosystems by Beth Savan (Perseus Press, 1992)

A Handful of Dirt by Raymond Bial (Walker Publishing Company, Inc.; 2000)

How a Plant Grows by Bobbie Kalman (Crabtree Publishing Company, 1997)

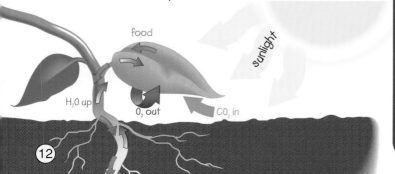

Phenomenal Photosynthesis
(Constructing a Model)

Help students understand the amazing chemical change that takes place during photosynthesis by constructing this colorful model. Begin by telling students that all substances are made of *molecules* (the smallest particle of a substance) and that molecules are made up of even smaller particles called *atoms* that can combine to form new substances. Point out that water (H_2O), for example, is made up of two atoms of hydrogen and one atom of oxygen. On the board, illustrate a water molecule and a carbon dioxide molecule as shown on the example reproducible.

Next, give each pair of students a copy of page 19, a glue stick, and hole-punched paper circles in the following colors and numbers: black (12), red (36), light blue (24). Direct students' attention to the equation on page 19. Identify it as the chemical equation for *photosynthesis* (the food-making process of plants). Explain that each part of the equation represents different molecules: on the left, six molecules of carbon dioxide (6 CO_2) and six molecules of water (6 H_2O); on the right, one molecule of sugar ($C_6H_{12}O_6$) and six molecules of oxygen (6 O_2). Point out to students that in photosynthesis the molecules of carbon, oxygen, and hydrogen are not used up—like fuel in a car—but combine to form new substances, including water, carbon dioxide, and sugar (glucose). Then have students complete page 19 as directed.

Give Me Light!
(Experiment, Making Observations)

Remind students that plants must have light to make food by conducting the following experiment. Gather a healthy green plant, paper clips, and four squares of black construction paper. Clip two paper squares to each of two plant leaves so that one square covers the top of the leaf and the other square covers the bottom. Then place the plant in a sunny window, watering as needed. After a week or so, remove the paper squares and ask students to compare the covered and uncovered leaves *(the covered leaves should have yellowed and may have started to shrivel, whereas the uncovered leaves remained green)*. With the leaves still uncovered, place the plant near the window for another week or so. Afterward, have students again observe the plant's leaves *(the leaves that had been covered should become green again)*. Help students conclude that *chlorophyll* (the green substance in plants) works with energy from the sun to help carbon dioxide and water combine to make a plant's food. If the plant can't make food, it eventually will die.

Follow up by having students try a variation of this experiment at home. Suggest that they turn a plastic dishpan or a metal pot upside down on a section of grass in their backyards for one week to observe similar results.

Here Comes the Sun...
(Identifying and Describing the Effects of Sunlight)

The sun helps plants make their own food, which in turn helps animals and humans who eat the plants. But can too much sun be bad for living things? Brainstorm with students a list of positive *and* negative effects of sunlight, listing students' responses on the board in two different columns. Or have groups of students research the positive and negative effects. Afterward, give each child a white paper plate, two sheets of lined paper, a compass, scissors, glue, and markers in the following colors: yellow, orange, and red. Direct her to use the markers to color the plate's front and back outer edges to make them resemble the sun's glowing rays. Also direct her to use the compass to trace and cut out two five-inch circles from lined paper, glue a circle to the center of each side of the plate, and then label the sides as shown. Have students use the lists on the board to help them write a descriptive paragraph on each side of the plate, writing one paragraph about the sun's positive effects and the other about the negative. If desired, suggest that students include additional effects they think of, including preventive measures. Then hang students' projects from the ceiling to create a sun-dazzling display!

Positive effects
- provides light
- provides warmth
- provides solar energy
- helps green plants grow and make food
- helps water evaporate
- helps grow plants for food

Negative effects
- can cause skin cancer
- can cause heat stroke
- can damage the eyes if looked at directly
- can contribute to drought
- can damage outer surfaces of some materials
- can burn the skin

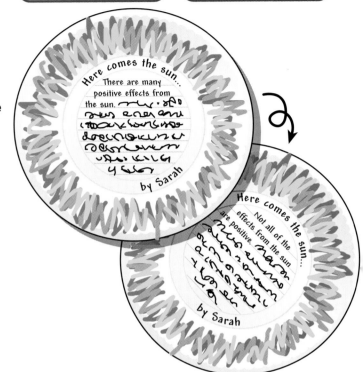

It's Raining Water Facts!
(Experiment, Researching Water Facts)

How essential is water to plants? Help students answer this question by having them first observe a simple experiment and then research interesting facts that create a refreshing rain-shower display. Place two bean plants (approximately the same size) in a sunny area. Water one plant as needed. Give the other plant no water. Over a period of two weeks, have students observe what happens (*the plant given no water should wilt and begin to die*).

Next, gather books about water and divide students into groups of five. Direct each student to scour the books for at least three interesting facts about water that are different from those collected by other group members. Next, provide each group with scissors, a copy of the rain-drop pattern on page 20, and one sheet each of white, light blue, and gray construction paper. Have each child use the pattern to trace three large paper raindrop shapes. Then she cuts them out and labels each one with a different fact and her initials. Using a hole puncher and paper clips, hang the cutouts at different heights from netting suspended from a corner ceiling. On another sheet of paper, have each student write two statements (one true, one false) about any of her facts. Collect students' papers; then use their statements to create a fun quiz that student pairs can complete as they walk through the shower of facts searching for answers!

Water is used over and over again and is never used up.

LS

Most of the earth's water is salty. Only about 3% is fresh.

SG

A tomato is about 95% water!

NM

Movin' On Up!
(Observing the Cohesiveness of Water)

How can water overcome gravity and rise from a plant's roots to stems and leaves that may be hundreds of feet in the air? Let this interesting experiment explain how. Divide students into groups. Provide each group of students with a five-ounce cup filled with water, a paper towel, and about 25 pennies. Ask students to estimate how many pennies can be added to the cup before water spills over the top edge. Next, have the group carefully add one penny at a time to the cup and observe what happens *(the water forms a bulge that rises above the cup's rim)*. Explain that the bulge represents water's *cohesiveness,* or ability to stick together. Tell students that the cohesiveness of water molecules is an important factor in *transpiration,* the movement of water through a plant. Point out that scientists believe that as plants evaporate extra water through their *stomata* (tiny holes in their leaves), the entire column of water in a plant's stem is pulled upward through its xylem tubes. Ask students to imagine the cohesiveness of water being strong enough to pull a column of water upward *300 feet* to the top of a redwood tree! To help students better understand the process of transpiration, have each one complete a copy of page 21 as directed.

Watching Plants Work Up a Sweat
(Experiment)

Do plants actually sweat? You bet! Demonstrate how to make this happen by using this simple experiment. First, ask students if they believe that plants sweat. After hearing their responses, explain that during *transpiration* (the movement of water through a plant), plants allow unused water to escape through the stomata on their leaves. Then share that on a hot day, a corn plant can release about a gallon of water! Introduce the experiment by telling students that they will be testing to find out how much water can be given off by common houseplants. Ask student volunteers to bring in a variety of same-sized potted plants. Water the plants evenly; then enclose each one in a large resealable plastic bag and place them in a sunny place. After several hours, have students observe the water droplets that have condensed inside the bags and note whether some plants "sweated" more than others.

Suitable Soil Substitute?
(Experiment, Making Observations)

How essential is soil for growing healthy land plants? Poll students to get their thoughts. Next, ask students whether they think plants could grow just as well in water as in soil. After hearing their thoughts, introduce the term *hydroponics,* the science of growing plants in a solution of water and minerals. Then conduct the experiment below and have students observe the results. Afterward, help them conclude that to be healthy, plants need the soil's nutrients (which they get when their roots absorb water), and that if this does not happen, the nutrients must be supplied artificially. Follow up by having students suggest circumstances in which using hydroponics to grow plants could be better than the traditional way *(to conserve water and space, and to grow plants year round).*

Water

Water With Miracle-Gro

Materials: 1 clear plastic cup filled with soil (not commercial), 2 small resealable plastic bags, black permanent marker, 3 lima bean seeds, 2 paper towels, plain water, water mixed with Miracle-Gro® Plant Food according to package directions, measuring spoon

Steps:
1. Plant a seed in the cup. Add enough water to dampen the soil.
2. Place a folded paper towel inside each plastic bag. Place a seed between the towel and the bag so it can be seen.
3. Label one bag "Water" and the other "Water With Miracle-Gro." Dampen the towels in each bag with water from the appropriate source.
4. Place the cup and bags in a sunny place and observe them for ten days. Add water as needed to keep the soil and towels damp.

(All the seeds should germinate and grow. The seed in the bag receiving Miracle-Gro should grow more than the one in the bag that is not.)

Seeking Soil Sources
(Research)

Send students digging for the sources of soil with this cooperative research activity. First, gather books about soil. Next, explain to students that soil is constantly being formed and destroyed and that the rate at which this happens depends on the climate. For example, soil forms slowly in places where the ground is frozen and rapidly where it is warm and wet. Announce that it takes 500 years for nature to create one inch of topsoil! Ask students where they think new soil comes from. After hearing the responses, divide students into groups of four and have them research the sources of soil *(sun, air, water, and other environmental forces that erode rocks).* Then give each group a 12" x 18" sheet of light-colored paper, a 9" x 12" sheet of colorful paper, scissors, glue, a ruler, and markers. Have the groups follow the steps below to record their work and then share it with the class. If desired, treat your researchers to a delicious snack of "dirt" (see the recipe below) as they listen to the reports!

Sources of Soil
by Carmen, Jake, Tia, and Ned

Wind | Ice
Animals | Machines | Plants

1. From the smaller sheet of paper, cut four-inch squares (one for each soil source found). Label each square accordingly.
2. Arrange the squares attractively on the larger sheet of paper; then label the larger sheet "Sources of Soil."
3. Glue the top edge of each square to the larger sheet of paper to form flaps.
4. On the paper under each flap, write a description (or draw a picture) illustrating how that source produces soil.

Delicious "Dirt"
1 large package Oreo® cookies, crushed
1 large package chocolate instant pudding
Gummy Worm candies®
small clear plastic cups
plastic spoons

Mix pudding according to package directions. In each cup, alternate layers of pudding and crushed cookies to make a total of four layers. Add a candy worm and serve.

Erosion...A Moving Experience
(Demonstration, Art)

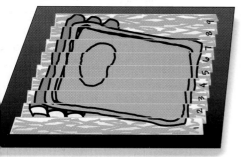
Before

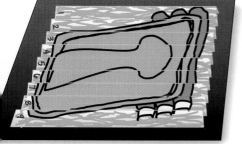
After

What is erosion? Help students answer this question by simulating what happens when rain falls on loose soil. Place a handful of loose soil on a cookie sheet. Poke holes in the top of a plastic milk jug opposite its handle. Fill the jug half full of water. Take the materials outside along with a stack of about three same-sized textbooks. Position one end of the cookie sheet on the stack of books so that the cookie sheet forms a 45 degree angle with the ground. Have a student hold the jug about two feet above the cookie sheet and sprinkle water until the jug is empty. Afterward, ask students the following questions: What happened when water was sprinkled on the cookie sheet? *(Much of the soil ran off the cookie sheet.)* What could keep the soil from washing away? *(Planting grass to hold the soil in place.)* Also ask students to name another force that can move soil from one place to another *(wind)*. Together, help students define *soil erosion* (the wearing, washing, or blowing away of soil by water or wind).

Back inside, pair students. Give each pair two 9" x 12" sheets of white paper, one 18" x 24" sheet of tagboard, an 18-inch square of black paper, a ruler, scissors, glue, and crayons or markers. Guide the pairs through the steps below to create a unique before-and-after scene of the demonstration.

Steps:
1. One partner turns her 9" x 12" sheet of paper vertically and colors it to show the demonstration scene, including how the soil looked before being sprinkled with water. The other partner colors her sheet to show the demonstration scene, including how the soil looked afterward.
2. Each partner draws eight vertical lines at one-inch intervals on her drawing, as shown, numbering the sections from left to right sequentially, and then cuts them into nine strips.
3. Each pair draws 17 similar lines at one-inch intervals on its tagboard and then folds it accordion-style along the lines.
4. Each pair glues the accordion tagboard's folded edges to the black paper square.
5. One partner at a time glues her strips to the raised sides of the accordion tagboard, gluing the *before* strips in order to the *left* side of each section and the *after* strips in order to the *right* side.
6. View the *before* scene from one angle and the *after* scene from the other.

Putting Soil to the (Filter) Test
(Demonstration, Making Observations)

Use soil as a filter? You betcha! This simple test demonstrates how soil cleans water as it passes through the earth's layers. Gather a soil sample, small rocks, a lidded glass jar three-fourths full of a mixture of soil and water, a paper towel, a clear plastic bottle, a black marker, and scissors. Cut off the top third of the bottle and turn it upside down in its bottom section to form a funnel. Line the funnel with a paper towel and layer first the rocks, then the soil in the funnel. Next, hold up the jar and shake it. Tell students that the dirty water represents rain mixing with loose soil. Remove the lid and slowly pour half the dirty water into the funnel. As you do, explain that this is what happens when a rain-soil mixture soaks into the ground. When the water has finished dripping, label the top of the plastic bottle "Filter," the bottom of the bottle "After," and the jar "Before." Have students compare the water before and after it was filtered *(the water after filtering should be noticeably cleaner)*. Help students conclude that the soil's *horizons* (layers) filter dirt from water as it soaks into the ground. If desired, make a copy of the funnel-shaped pattern on page 20 for each student, having her describe her observations and conclusion on it.

Hungry for Air!
(Experiment, Making Observations)

Will a plant starve if not exposed to air? Let students find out by conducting this simple test. Obtain two plants approximately the same size; then gather a glass jar (large enough to cover one plant), duct tape, and a ruler. Measure and water the plants; then place them on a desktop in a sunny area (not direct sunlight). Turn the jar upside down over one plant and use duct tape to seal the jar to the desktop. Have students observe the plants for about two weeks and then measure them again *(the plant under the jar should show no growth; the other plant should grow slightly)*. Help students understand that because green plants require carbon dioxide to carry on *photosynthesis* (their food-making process) and if CO_2 is not present, the plant stops making food. Conclude by having students infer what would happen to the plant if the jar were not removed *(the plant would eventually starve)*.

A Plant's Gotta Breathe!
(Game)

Review the process of respiration in plants with an active team game that gives students' own respiratory systems a wonderful workout! In advance, cut two large plant outlines from green bulletin board paper and mount them on opposite sides of the chalkboard. On the board between the cutouts, write the following equation: sugar + oxygen —> carbon dioxide + water + energy. Next, label two sets of five sticky notes each with a different part of the equation. Divide students into two teams. Give each team a set of sticky notes and have it line up at an equal distance away from and facing one of the cutouts. Then guide students through the steps below to help them remember what happens during plant respiration. At game's end, no doubt students will agree that respiration is hard work!

Steps:
1. At your signal, Player 1 on each team runs the note labeled "sugar" to the board, places it *on* the leaf of his team's cutout, and then tags Player 2 on his team.
2. Player 2 places the "oxygen" note *on* the leaf and tags Player 3.
3. Player 3 places "carbon dioxide" *near* the leaf and tags Player 4.
4. Player 4 places "water" *near* the carbon dioxide note and tags Player 5.
5. Player 5 places "energy" anywhere *on* the cutout and tags Player 6.
6. Player 6 runs up and collects all five of his team's notes and returns them to the team so the process can begin again with the next player. Declare the first team to rotate through all its players in this manner the winner.
7. Together with students, conclude by using the equation to review the process of plant respiration: oxygen enters the plant through *stomata* (small openings) in its leaves, where it combines with food (sugar) to form carbon dioxide and water (which are released into the air) and energy (which is set free or used to perform the plant's activities).

Name _____

Phenomenal Photosynthesis

Key

C = carbon (black)
O = oxygen (red)
H = hydrogen (light blue)

Photosynthesis is the food-making process of green plants. To make their own food, plants need light, carbon dioxide, and water. A plant's leaves trap the energy from sunlight in a green substance called *chlorophyll* to create sugar (its food) and release oxygen (a waste product). Create a model of this food-making process of plants by using the materials provided by your teacher and the directions below. Then answer the questions by writing a number in each blank.

Directions:

1. Look at the four different shapes shown below: air bubbles, drops of water, a sugar cube, and clouds.

2. Inside each **bubble,** glue one black paper circle (carbon atom) atop each carbon symbol. Glue one red paper circle (oxygen atom) atop each oxygen symbol. This creates six molecules of carbon dioxide.

3. Inside each **water drop,** glue one light blue paper circle (hydrogen atom) atop each hydrogen symbol. Glue one red paper circle (oxygen atom) atop each oxygen symbol. This creates six water molecules.

4. On the **sugar cube,** glue one black paper circle (carbon atom) atop each carbon symbol, one red paper circle (oxygen atom) atop each oxygen symbol, and one light blue paper circle (hydrogen atom) atop each hydrogen symbol. This creates one molecule of glucose.

5. Inside each **cloud shape,** glue a red paper circle (oxygen atom) atop each oxygen symbol. This creates six molecules of oxygen.

6. Use the key to label each paper circle with its symbol.

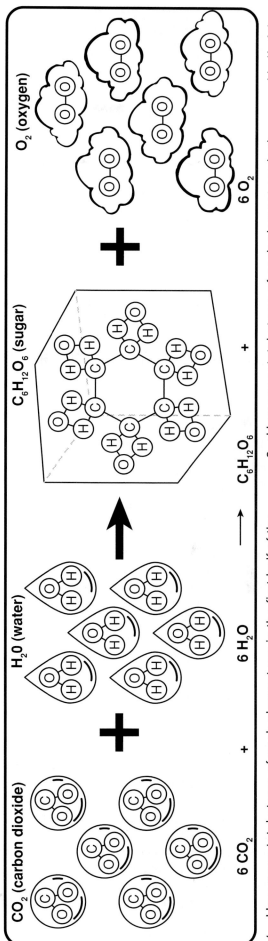

CO_2 (carbon dioxide)

H_2O (water)

$C_6H_{12}O_6$ (sugar)

O_2 (oxygen)

$6 CO_2$ + $6 H_2O$ ⟶ $C_6H_{12}O_6$ + $6 O_2$

1. How many total atoms of each element are in the first half of the equation?
   a. carbon = _____   b. oxygen = _____   c. hydrogen = _____

2. How many total atoms of each element are in the second half of the equation?
   a. carbon = _____   b. oxygen = _____   c. hydrogen = _____

©2000 The Education Center, Inc. • *Investigating Science • Plants* • TEC1733

Note to the teacher: Use with "Phenomenal Photosynthesis" on page 13.

Patterns
Use raindrop pattern with "It's Raining Water Facts!" on page 14.
Use funnel pattern with "Putting Soil to the (Filter) Test" on page 17.

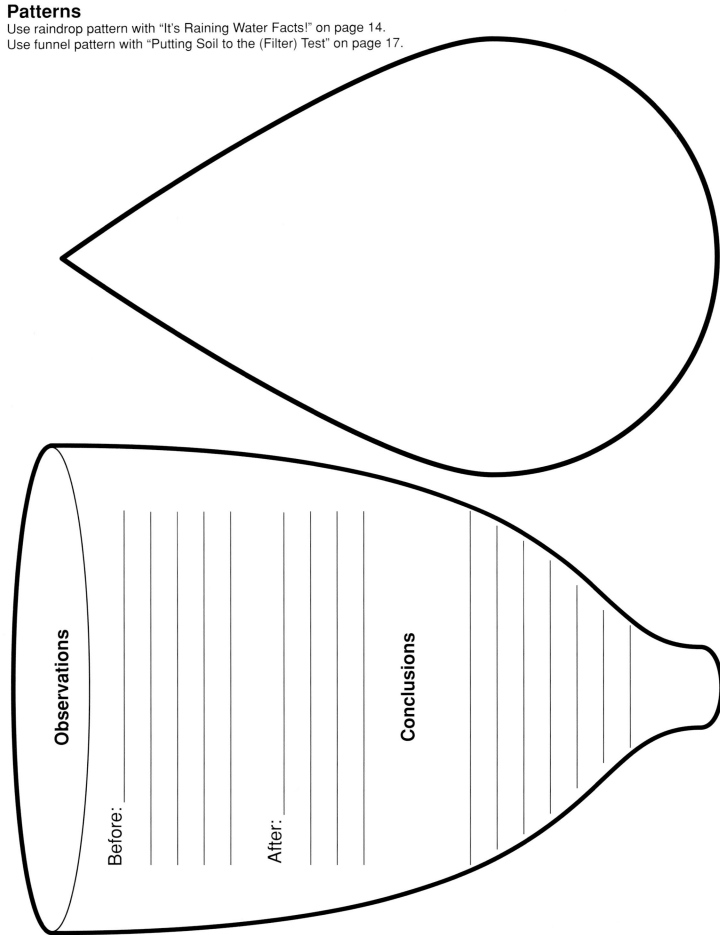

Observations

Before: _____

After: _____

Conclusions

Travelin' Along With Transpiration

Transpiration is the flow of water through a plant. But what path does the water take? Follow the directions in Part One and Part Two below to discover the water's path *and* learn lots more about transpiration and plants.

Part One: Read about transpiration in a science book or an encyclopedia. Then complete each sentence below by writing a word from the word list in each blank. Also write the number of the matching sentence in each circle in the diagram. Use each word and number only once.

Word List

xylem vessels	stem
sun	absorbs
transpiration	cool
roots	stomata
evaporates	water

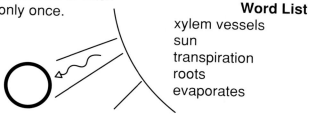

1. As the _____ warms the water inside a plant's leaves, _____ occurs. This warming makes much of the water change into water vapor that _____.

2. The water vapor escapes into the atmosphere through the _____ in the leaves.

3. The water vapor _____ heat as it escapes, which helps the inside of the leaves _____.

4. To replace the lost water, _____ draw up more _____.

5. It travels up the _____ and along the veins of leaves through tiny tubes called _____.

Part Two: Complete each analogy below by choosing the appropriate word(s) from the list provided. Use a science book or an encyclopedia for help. *Hint: Not all words will be used.*

arteries and veins
fan
perspiration
vitamins and minerals
digestion
precipitation
pores
stomach
oxygen, hydrogen, and nitrogen
meat, cheese, and bread

1. Transpiration is to plants as _____ is to humans.

2. Stomata are to plants as _____ are to humans.

3. Water, carbon dioxide, and light are to photosynthesis as _____ are to a sandwich.

4. Xylem vessels are to plants as _____ are to humans.

5. Nutrients are to plants as _____ are to humans.

Bonus Box: On the back of this page, write an analogy of your own about plants.

Note to the teacher: Use with "Movin' On Up!" on page 15.

21

Respiration And Photosynthesis: A "F-air" Trade

Directions: Carefully read the paragraphs below to learn how dependent people and plants are on one another for oxygen and carbon dioxide. Then, in the outline on the left, explain why the exchange of these gases is important to people. In the outline on the right, explain why the exchange of these gases is important to plants. Use your own words to write your explanations.

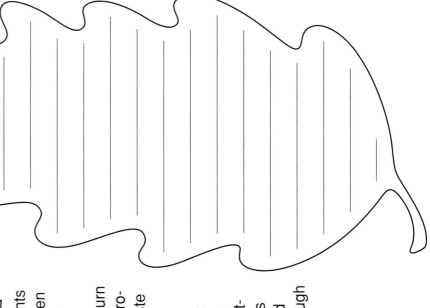

carbon dioxide CO_2

oxygen O_2

In the process known as *respiration*, both plants and humans take in oxygen. Plants take in oxygen (through tiny openings in their leaves called *stomata*) and use it to get the energy they need to burn food. People take in oxygen to help them burn digested food and get energy. Both processes produce carbon dioxide, which is given off as a waste product.

Plants make their own food in the process known as *photosynthesis*. To make food, a plant takes in carbon dioxide through its stomata. The carbon dioxide is used by *chlorophyll* (green matter) in the plant's leaves along with water from its roots and energy from sunlight to make food and oxygen. The oxygen is released into the air through the stomata as a waste product. Unlike plants, people cannot make their own food.

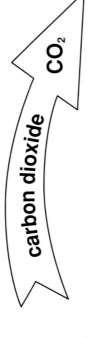

Bonus Box: Yeast and bacteria use *anaerobic* respiration. Use a dictionary to learn the meaning of anaerobic. Then write a sentence on the back of this page explaining what anaerobic respiration is.

©2000 The Education Center, Inc. • *Investigating Science* • *Plants* • TEC1733 • Key p. 48

Name _____

Oops! What's Missing?

The scientists at Essential Plant Needs, Inc., know that land plants need light, water, soil, and air to be healthy. Help these scientists keep up the good work by identifying which important element (light, water, soil, or air) is missing for the plant in each situation below. *Hint: Some may be missing more than one element.*

Case #1
Plant in sunny area and soil-filled, glass case equipped with removable stopper for watering
Needs _____

Case #2
Plant outside in sunlight in pebble-filled container where watered by sprinkler twice daily
Needs _____

Case #3
Plant in soil-filled container left under leaky water pipe in corner of windowless warehouse
Needs _____

Case #4
Windblown black plastic bag completely covering leaves of garden plant
Needs _____

Case #5
Plant with burlap bag over its soil and roots fell off back of truck in desert
Needs _____

Case #6
Plant in soil-filled container sealed inside clear plastic wrap left on back step of house by movers
Needs _____

Case #7
Uprooted plant tossed between two rocks in stream
Needs _____

Case #8
Plant buried under three inches of soil by dog digging hole in flower bed
Needs _____

Case #9
Plant in container of gravel left outside on uncovered patio
Needs _____

Case #10
Plant in container of potting soil left outside under large canopy
Needs _____

Bonus Box: Illustrate one of the cases above on the back of this paper.

Seeds

Sow some seeds of learning with the following original ideas, activities, and reproducibles.

Background for the Teacher

- *Seeds* are the parts of plants that make new plants.
- There are two groups of seed plants: *angiosperms* and *gymnosperms.*
- Angiosperms—flowering plants—are the largest group of seed plants. Angiosperm seeds are enclosed in the fruit of the plant.
- Gymnosperms are trees and shrubs that usually produce cones. The seeds are inside the cones.
- Seeds come in all different sizes, but the size of the seed has no relationship to how big that plant will be. Giant redwoods grow from seeds no bigger than 1/16 inch.
- There are three parts to a seed: an *embryo,* a *food supply,* and a *seed coat.*
- The embryo is a miniature plant within the seed.
- The food supply is where the plant gets its energy until photosynthesis begins.
- The seed coat protects the seed.
- *Cotyledons,* or leaf-like structures, absorb and digest the food stored in the seed. The embryo has at least one cotyledon.
- Angiosperms have either one or two cotyledons. Gymnosperms have from two to eight cotyledons.
- Angiosperms are called either *monocots* (monocotyledons), having one cotyledon, or *dicots* (dicotyledons), having two cotyledons.

Seed Sort
(Sorting, Art)

Although seeds are very different from one another, their differences help them achieve the same goal of making new plants. From a local garden center, buy 10 to 12 seed packets of various fruits and vegetables. Then divide the class into six groups and provide each group with a paper plate and a few seeds from each packet. Ask students to sort the seeds in different ways according to their characteristics (such as by size or by shape). After groups have sorted the seeds, ask them if they think these characteristics might help the seeds make new plants. *(For example, a dandelion seed is light with a fluffy white covering attached to it. This covering helps the dandelion seed travel to a different area, carried by the wind. Explain to students that each seed has different characteristics, but that each difference helps that seed disperse, or scatter, and eventually germinate, or sprout.)* Have one student from each team share the group's observations.

Afterward, give each student a 5" x 7" piece of poster board and a sampling of seeds. Have each student think about the characteristics of her seeds and draw a garden-related picture, blending her real seeds into the picture (for instance, she might use seeds for a bird's wings or for the body of an insect). Display the pictures on a bulletin board titled "Can You See the Seeds?"

Literature for Growing Minds

The Dandelion Seed by Joseph Anthony (DAWN Publications, 1997)
From Seed to Plant by Gail Gibbons (Holiday House, Inc.; 1991)
The Magic School Bus® Plants Seeds: A Book About How Living Things Grow by Joanna Cole (Scholastic Inc., 1995)
Seeds and Seedlings (Nature Close-Up series) by Elaine Pascoe (Blackbirch Press, 1997)
A Weed Is a Flower: The Life of George Washington Carver by Aliki (Econo-Clad Books, 1999)

Seeds...Everywhere!
(Experiment, Estimating From a Sample)

A grocery's produce department can supply the materials for a tasty study of seeds. In advance, create a list of about 10 to 15 seedy fruits and vegetables, such as squash, tomatoes, and apples. Solicit parents' help in gathering the listed produce. To begin the lesson, display the fruits and vegetables and ask students how many seeds they think are in each one. Record their guesses on the board. Then pair students, providing each pair with the materials listed and a copy of the steps below. Have students follow the steps to determine the number of seeds (or an estimate of the number) found in each kind of fruit or vegetable.

After students determine the number of seeds each fruit or vegetable contains, have the class compare the counts with their earlier guesses. Ask students why they think there are so many seeds inside fruits and vegetables. *(Having lots of seeds increases the chance of one of those seeds successfully becoming a new plant. Also, being in the fruit of the plant helps disperse the seeds when the fruit is taken from the plant and eaten.)* As a tasty follow-up, provide juice and fresh fruits and vegetables as a snack.

Materials needed for each pair:
1 fruit or vegetable, 1 paper plate, 1 plastic knife

Steps for each pair:
1. Carefully *quarter*—or cut into four equal-sized sections—the fruit or vegetable.
2. If possible, count every seed. Record the number.
3. If there are many seeds, count the seeds in only one of the quarters. Then estimate the total number of seeds in the entire fruit or vegetable by multiplying by four. Record the number.

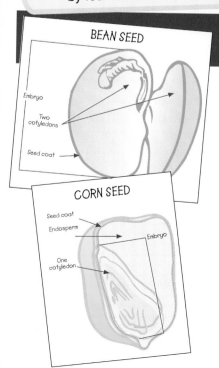

BEAN SEED

Embryo

Two cotyledons

Seed coat

CORN SEED

Seed coat

Endosperm

Embryo

One cotyledon

What's Inside?
(Experiment, Dissecting Seeds)

Have you and your students ever wondered what's inside a seed? Use the following seed-comparing activity to satisfy that curiosity! Give each child a cup of water, a toothpick, two lima bean seeds, and two corn seeds. Have her place her seeds in the water and soak them overnight. The next day, use the background information on page 24 to discuss with students the parts of a seed—the embryo, the food supply, and the seed coat—and the role of each part. Next, have each student carefully split open one of her lima bean seeds with a toothpick and then use her fingers to pinch off the outer covering of a corn seed. Instruct the children to sketch what each seed reveals, showing how the seeds are similar and how they are different. Have students share what they observed. Next, explain to your students what cotyledons are and discuss the difference between monocots and dicots (see the background information). Have students identify the number of cotyledons in each seed, identifying it as a monocot or a dicot. *(The lima bean seed is a dicot, and the corn seed is a monocot.)* For another activity on monocots and dicots, see the reproducible on page 27.

Collecting Coniferous Cones
(Identifying Cones)

If you've got coniferous trees in your town, then you've got cones. So grab a container and check under every pine, fir, and spruce! Before beginning the activity, collect a supply of different cones. (Make sure the cones are dry and free of insects before bringing them into the classroom.) Provide each student with paper and crayons or colored pencils. Then divide the class into six groups. Give each group an assortment of cones and access to an appropriate reference book such as *National Audubon Society First Field Guide: Trees* by Brian Cassie (Scholastic Inc., 1999). Direct each group to identify the tree each of its cones came from. Then have each student choose a cone, write down the name of the tree it's from, and draw a picture of the tree, its leaves (the needles), its cones, and its seeds. Finally, share with students that the seeds of coniferous trees are found inside the (female) cones. Hold up a cone and ask students where they think the seeds would be located. Ask students why they think coniferous trees might keep their seeds inside cones. *(Cones are how coniferous trees protect and store their seeds. The seeds lie along the inside of the scales of the cone. When they become ripe, the scales open and drop the usually winged seeds.)* Display the finished projects on a wall titled "Collecting Coniferous Cones."

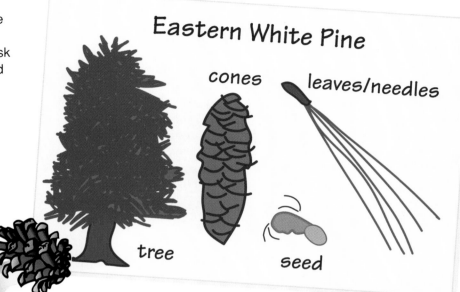

A Nutty Seed
(Making a Cookbook)

Celebrate one sensational seed—the peanut—with your students. Point out to students that different seeds are eaten by people and by animals, but for many people, the peanut is the most popular! (Americans eat more peanuts each year than almonds, hazelnuts, and walnuts combined.) Explain that the peanut's popularity exploded when a man named George Washington Carver discovered more than 300 uses for it. Then share more about the peanut and Carver's life by reading aloud *The Life and Times of the Peanut* by Charles Micucci (Houghton Mifflin Company, 1997). Afterward, discuss with students why the peanut crop was so important to farmers during Carver's life. *(In 1905, the boll weevil destroyed almost half of the cotton crop, so Carver encouraged many farmers to give peanuts a try. Peanuts were not only easy to grow but they also had many uses and improved the soil.)*

Next, have each student bring in a copy of his favorite recipe that uses peanuts (or peanut butter). Then make a peanut-shaped class cookbook with student recipes, titling it "Peanuts Aplenty." To make the booklet, cut out a peanut shape from a piece of tagboard. Using that piece as a template, trace and cut out a back cover from tagboard and enough notebook paper for all of the recipes. Have each student copy his peanut recipe onto a peanut-shaped page and decorate that page. When everyone has finished, decorate and assemble the booklet. Then hole-punch the left side and bind the booklet together with yarn. Have kids review the recipes and vote on their favorite. If desired, prepare and share with students the recipe they chose and sample just how super this seed really is.

Name _____

Cotyledon Confusion

Monocot	Dicot

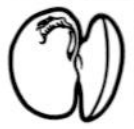

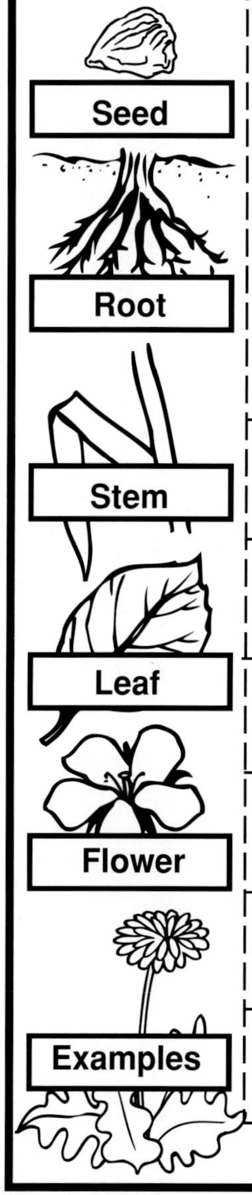

Hannah, a hyper horticulturist, was in a huge hurry when she made this chart. She had hardly finished when she realized all of her research was mixed up! Help Hannah get things back in order by following the directions below. Use reference materials for help.

Directions:
1. Cut out the dashed rectangle, leaving the frame intact. Then cut apart the information boxes.
2. Color the frame and glue it to a 9" x 12" sheet of colorful construction paper.
3. Read the information in each box. Decide which boxes fit into each column—*monocot* (one seed leaf) or *dicot* (two seed leaves)—and each row (seed, root, stem, etc.).
4. When the information boxes are in place, glue them onto your paper.

Seed
- two *cotyledons*, or seed "leaves"
- one *cotyledon*, or seed "leaf"

Root
- broad leaves with branching veins
- one main root (*taproot*) with very small roots branching off of it
- similarly sized, branching roots

Stem
- both woody and *herbaceous* (nonwoody) stems with *vascular bundles* (tubes through which sap travels) in rings
- usually *herbaceous* (nonwoody) stems with scattered *vascular bundles* (tubes through which sap travels)

Leaf
- petals are in fours or fives; petals and *sepals* (leaflike structures below the flower) are easy to tell apart
- narrow leaves with parallel veins

Flower
- petals are in threes; *sepals* (leaflike structures below the flower) and petals are hard to tell apart

Examples
- peanut, bean, violet, maple tree
- iris, grass, lily, palm tree, corn

©2000 The Education Center, Inc. • *Investigating Science • Plants* • TEC1733 • Key p. 48

Note to the teacher: Provide each student with scissors, a 9" x 12" sheet of construction paper, crayons or markers, glue, and access to appropriate reference materials.

27

Name_____   *Reading for details*

Peeking at Packets

Seed packets are packed with piles of information about planting! Use the seed packet shown below to answer the questions that follow.

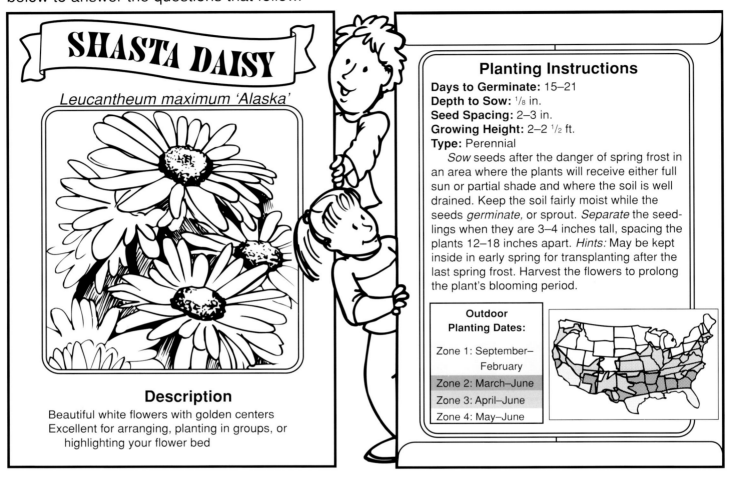

1. What is the fewest number of days in which this seed might germinate? _____
2. If the seeds are planted on March 3, what is the earliest date that germination would be expected? _____
3. How tall can the plants be expected to grow? _____
4. What is the scientific name of the Shasta daisy? _____
5. Will this flower grow again next year? _____
6. How much sunlight should the Shasta daisy receive? _____
7. If you lived in Michigan, what would be the earliest month you could plant the seed?
   _____
8. If you lived in Florida, what would be the latest month you could plant the seed?
   _____
9. During germination, how much water should the Shasta daisy seed receive? _____
10. What activity will prolong the flower's blooming period? _____
11. How tall should the seedlings be when you separate them? _____
12. True or false? The Shasta daisy seeds should be sown 2–3 inches deep. _____

Bonus Box: Make up your own plant. Draw a seed packet and a picture of the flower on the back of this paper. Be sure to include the planting instructions for your flower.

Planning and Plotting

Gordy Griffith, a local gardener, is helping your class plant its very own vegetable garden! He's provided the class with a 9' x 12' plot that has been equally divided into 3' x 3' sections and seeds for six different vegetables. Gordy has also given you some pointers: There should be only one kind of vegetable planted in each section of the plot with the maximum number of vegetables that will fit into it. No vegetable should be planted on a section border. After doing some research and taking notes, you and your classmates are ready to begin!

Directions:

1. Using the research notes, decide where to plant each vegetable and how much of it to plant.
2. Record the information about the placement and number of plants in the blanks below. Then show the information by drawing a picture in the plot provided.
3. On the back of this sheet, write a brief paragraph explaining why you planted the garden the way you did.

Research Notes

Green Onions
- Grow in partial shade
- Plant 1" apart, 8" between rows
- Harvest when tops are 6" tall

Lettuce

- Grow in partial shade
- Plant 8" apart, 18" between rows
- Harvest when heads are above soil

Carrots
- Grow where they can get morning sun
- Plant 3" apart, 18" between rows
- Edible root 3" to 8" long

Beans

- Grow in full sun
- Grow on a tall pole for support
- Plant 4" apart, 20" between rows

Tomatoes

- Grow in full sun
- Grow in tall tomato cage for support
- Plant 18" apart, 3' between rows

Corn

- Grow in full sun
- Plant 12" apart, 3' between rows
- Most grow about 9' tall

Planting Hints: Grow the taller plants in the back or on the sides of your garden if you don't want their shade to interfere with other plants. The back of your garden is on the north side. (**Note:** ' = foot   " = inch.)

N

W   **E**

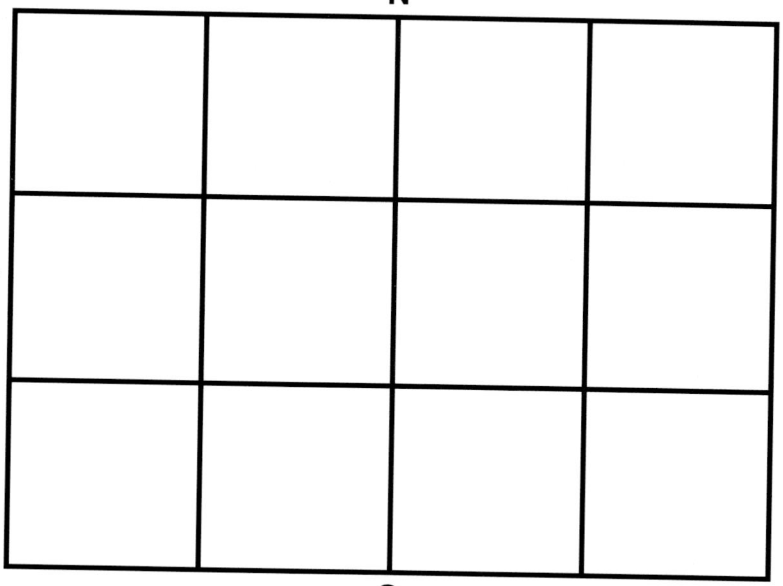

S

Green Onions
Sections Planted _____
Number of Rows _____
Plants in Each Row _____

Lettuce
Sections Planted _____
Number of Rows _____
Plants in Each Row _____

Carrots
Sections Planted _____
Number of Rows _____
Plants in Each Row _____

Beans
Sections Planted _____
Number of Rows _____
Plants in Each Row _____

Tomatoes
Sections Planted _____
Number of Rows _____
Plants in Each Row _____

Corn
Sections Planted _____
Number of Rows _____
Plants in Each Row _____

Life Cycles

Come full circle on your study of plant life cycles with this creative collection of experiments, activities, and reproducibles.

Background for the Teacher

- A *life cycle* is the process of growing, changing, reproducing, and dying. All plants and animals have life cycles.
- The life cycle of a plant consists of germinating, maturing, flowering, and reproducing.
- *Germination* takes place when a seed sprouts or begins to grow.
- The growth of a plant is affected by the water, nitrogen, and carbon cycles.
- *Water* transports nutrients through plants to help them grow.
- *Nitrogen* is used by plants to make protein, which is needed for healthy growth.
- *Carbon* exists in living things as the gas *carbon dioxide.*
- Plants absorb carbon dioxide through their leaves to make oxygen and carbohydrates, or a plant's food.

Life Cycle Selections

Dandelion Adventures by L. Patricia Kite (The Millbrook Press, Inc.; 1998)

A Dandelion's Life (Nature Upclose series) by John Himmelman (Children's Press, Inc.; 1999)

Fire: Friend or Foe by Dorothy Hinshaw Patent (Clarion Books, 1998)

From Seed to Sunflower (Lifecycles series) by Gerald Legg (Franklin Watts, Inc.; 1998)

What Is a Life Cycle? (Science of Living Things series) by Bobbie Kalman and Jacqueline Langille (Crabtree Publishing Company, 1998)

What Rot! Nature's Mighty Recycler by Elizabeth Ring (The Millbrook Press, Inc.; 1996)

Significant Cycles
(Research, Art)

Get your students thinking about the various cycles in nature that affect plant growth with this research-based art project. Use the background information on this page to discuss with students the important role that water, nitrogen, and carbon cycles play in the growth of plants. Next, divide students into groups of three, giving each group the following materials: three six-inch-diameter paper plates, one copy of page 34, scissors, crayons, glue, and a 9" x 12" sheet of green construction paper. Instruct each group to research the stages of each cycle discussed. Have the group then color and cut out the puzzle pieces on page 34 and use the information they learned to help arrange the pieces to show the complete stages of each cycle. Direct the group to glue each completed cycle onto the center of a paper plate as shown. Invite the group to decorate the edges of the plates to resemble colorful flowers. To complete its flowers, instruct the group to draw and cut out leaves and stems, using the green construc-tion paper. Display the finished flowers on a wall titled "Significant Cycles."

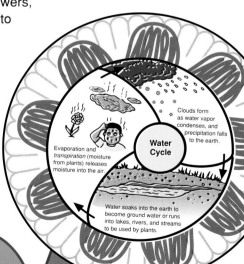

Clouds form as water vapor condenses, and precipitation falls to the earth.

Evaporation and *transpiration* (moisture from plants) releases moisture into the air.

Water Cycle

Water soaks into the earth to become ground water or runs into lakes, rivers, and streams to be used by plants.

One Dandy Life Story
(Identifying the Life Cycle of a Flower)

Further your study of the life cycle of plants with this dandy activity! Begin by reading a book about the life cycle of dandelions, such as *Dandelion Adventures* by L. Patricia Kite or *A Dandelion's Life* by John Himmelman (see page 30 for publishing information). Use the book as a springboard for discussing a plant's life cycle (germinating, maturing, flowering, and reproducing). Next, give each student a copy of page 35, one sheet of light-colored construction paper, scissors, and glue. Direct the student to cut out the boxes on page 35 and put them in order to show the dandelion's life cycle from beginning to end. Instruct each student to fold the sheet of construction paper in half lengthwise and then glue the boxes in order above the fold. Then have the student cut a sheet of notebook paper into six equal sections and glue each section below each box as shown. On each section, have the student write a description of what is happening in the picture above it, using the vocabulary words in that picture's box. Direct the student to underline these vocabulary words in his writing. Finally, have the student add a title and a decorative border to his paper. Display students' finished products on a bulletin board titled "One Dandy Life Story."

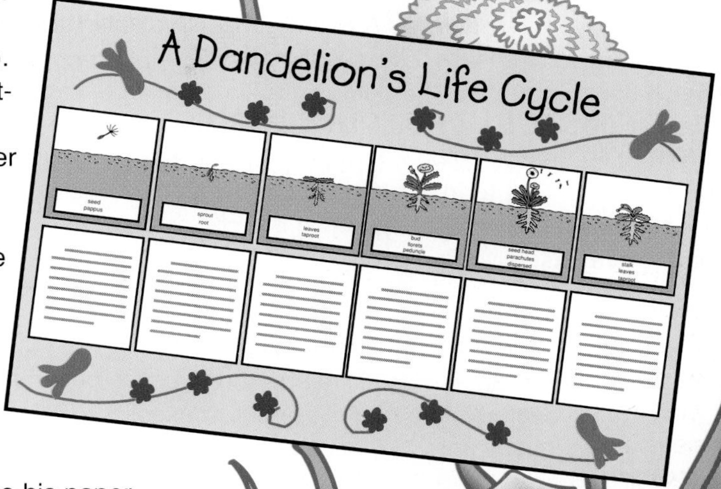

A Dandelion's Life Cycle

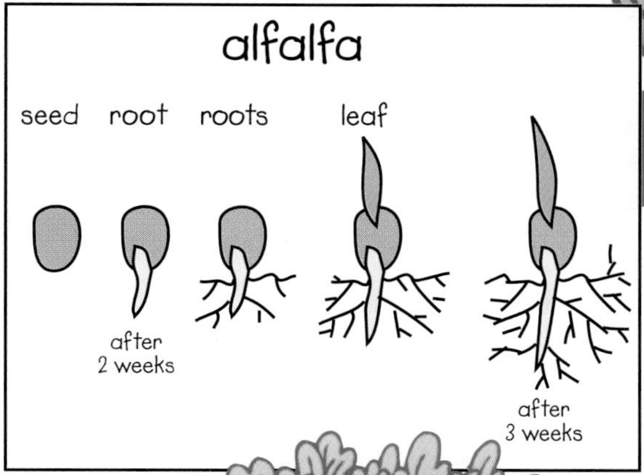

alfalfa

seed   root   roots   leaf

after 2 weeks

after 3 weeks

Sprouting With Character!
(Growing Sprouts, Art)

Sprout some interest in the life cycle of plants by having students grow their own sprouts. Before beginning the activity, gather for each student one-eighth to one-fourth teaspoon alfalfa sprout seeds; cotton; and a small container, such as a film canister, baby food jar, or small, clear plastic drinking cup. Next, explain to students that all plants follow the same life cycle. Share with students the life cycle of an alfalfa seed, shown at the left. Then give each student the materials listed. Have the student fill her container with cotton, wet the cotton with a small amount of water, and put her seeds on top of it. Place students' containers in a partly shady to sunny location. Make sure students keep the cotton moist. Direct each student to observe her seeds for the next few days, noticing the different stages of the life cycle *(germination and maturation)* taking place.

After the seeds have sprouted, give each student a variety of arts-and-crafts supplies and glue. Direct the student to create a sprout character—making a face on her container using the provided materials (the sprouts serve as the character's hair). If desired, instruct each student to label a sheet of paper with her sprout character's name, and the character's traits. Display students' characters and descriptions in a prominent place.
Warning: Do not allow students to eat the sprouts, and have them wash their hands after handling.

Propagating Plants
(Demonstration, Understanding Plant Propagation)

Is it possible for a plant to begin its life without starting from a seed? Answer this question for students with this demonstration on propagating plants. Ahead of time, gather a potato with developed eyes, an African violet plant, two branches from a hardy shrub, soil, two cups for each plant type, foil, and two rubber bands. (Two cuttings from each plant are used to ensure a successful experiment.) Follow the directions below to complete the demonstration. Afterward, explain to students that it is possible to grow a plant without starting with a seed. Point out that *propagation* is the growing of a new plant from part of an existing plant. One form of propagation is *cuttage*, or using part of a plant (usually the stem) and planting it in soil or water until it grows roots and eventually forms a new plant.

Directions:
1. Cut two pieces from the potato, each containing an eye.
2. Fill two cups about half full of soil and put each potato piece in a cup. Fill each cup the rest of the way with soil.
3. Cut two leaves from the African violet near the plant's stem.
4. Fill the cups with soil and plant one stem in each cup.
5. Fill two cups with water and cover the tops with foil. Use rubber bands to secure the foil.
6. Poke a small hole in each foil cup, sticking a shrub branch through it and into the water.
7. Water the plants in the soil and keep the water fresh for the shrub cuttings.
8. Observe for several weeks.

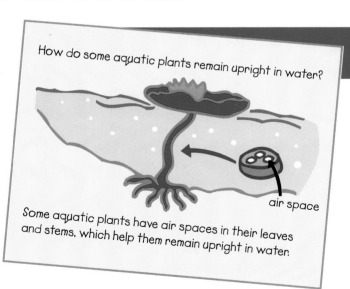

How do some aquatic plants remain upright in water?

air space

Some aquatic plants have air spaces in their leaves and stems, which help them remain upright in water.

Questions
Why do roses have thorns?
How do desert cacti survive with so little water?
How do flowers attract bees and other insects for pollination?
How do animals help spread seeds?
How are maple seeds dispersed?
How do some aquatic plants remain upright in water?
How do the roots of a mangrove tree help support it in water?
How do citrus plants protect themselves?
What does foxglove contain that deters insects and animals?
How does silica protect some grasses?

Clever Creatures
(Research, Making a Class Book)

Use this class activity to explore with your students the unique adaptations plants have developed to continue their life cycles. First, brainstorm with students the things people need and do to survive, such as wearing warm clothes and drinking plenty of water. Then discuss the things plants do in order to survive, such as storing water and fending off predators. Next, list the questions at the left on the board or on an overhead transparency. Read two or three of the questions together, and ask students to hypothesize answers. Discuss students' responses.

Divide the class into groups of two or three and give each group a 12" x 18" sheet of light-colored construction paper and markers. Have each group select a different question from the list to research. Direct the group to make a mini-poster of its question and answer, and then add a labeled illustration showing the plant's special adaptions. Invite each group to share its poster. Compile the posters into a big book, asking one student to create a cover. Bind the posters and cover and title it "Clever Creatures."

Take a Stand!
(Demonstration, Identifying Benefits of Forest Fires)

Are all forest fires bad? Pose this question to your students to assess their prior knowledge of the benefits of forest fires. Then make a line down the middle of your classroom with tape or string. At one end of the line, place a sign that reads "Forest fires are bad" and, at the other end, place one that reads "Forest fires are good." Have each student stand on the line to show her opinion about forest fires. *(Students will probably stand on the "bad" end.)* Ask student volunteers to share the reasons for their opinions.

Next, have students return to their seats. Share with them a book about forest fires, such as *Fire: Friend or Foe* by Dorothy Hinshaw Patent (see page 30 for publishing information). Then discuss the benefits of forest fires, such as clearing the way for new growth, providing nutrients essential for the development of new forests, and ensuring the survival of some species of animals. Remind students that forest fires are dangerous and should not be intentionally set. Then have each student stand on the line again to show her opinion. *(Students will probably stand more toward the middle, rather than the ends.)* Ask student volunteers to share whether or not their opinions have changed and why or why not. As a follow-up to this activity, have students complete "A Successful Succession of New Life" on page 36 to learn how fire is a part of a forest's growth.

Plant Succession by Andy

The Fire Stage

The Meadow Stage

The Thicket Stage

The Intermediate Forest Stage

The Mature Forest Stage

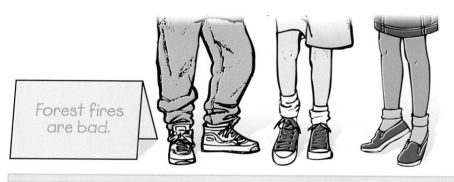

Forest fires are bad.

Example of project from page 36

The Many Faces of Decomposition
(Observing, Writing)

Help students discover the different agents of decomposition with this observation activity. In advance, gather pieces of various fruits and vegetables. Explain to students that when plants die, they *decompose,* or rot, and become part of the soil again. Further explain that the decomposition makes the soil richer and more fertile to help new plants grow. Ask students to imagine the heap of dead plants there would be if plants did not decompose! Next, read to students *What Rot! Nature's Mighty Recycler* by Elizabeth Ring (see page 30 for publishing information) to help them better understand this process. Then take students outside to place the gathered items around the schoolyard. Continue the activity by taking students outside every day or so to observe how each item has changed in size, shape, and color. Invite students to identify the causes of the changes, such as mold growth, bacteria, and small animals. Finally, have students write a descriptive paragraph about the decomposition of one of the plants. If desired, direct the student to publish her final copy on a colorful construction paper cutout of a fruit or vegetable.

Cycle Patterns

Use with "Significant Cycles" on page 30.

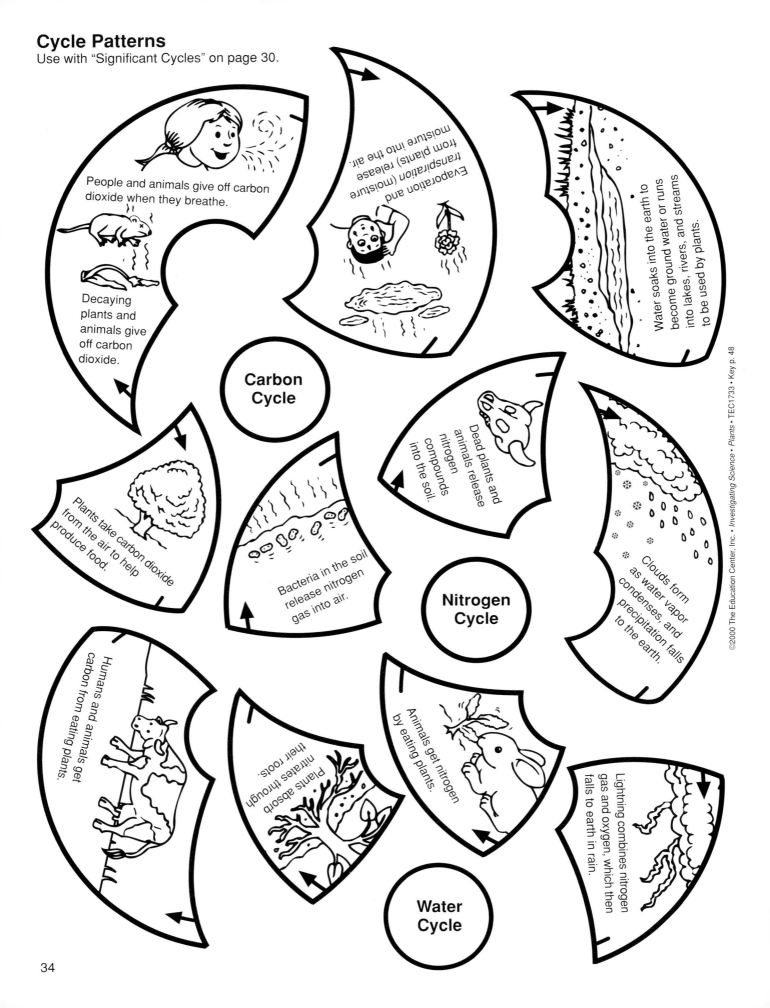

People and animals give off carbon dioxide when they breathe.

Decaying plants and animals give off carbon dioxide.

Evaporation and transpiration (moisture from plants) release moisture into the air.

Water soaks into the earth to become ground water or runs into lakes, rivers, and streams to be used by plants.

Carbon Cycle

Dead plants and animals release nitrogen compounds into the soil.

Plants take carbon dioxide from the air to help produce food.

Bacteria in the soil release nitrogen gas into air.

Clouds form as water vapor condenses, and precipitation falls to the earth.

Nitrogen Cycle

Humans and animals get carbon from eating plants.

Plants absorb nitrates through their roots.

Animals get nitrogen by eating plants.

Lightning combines nitrogen gas and oxygen, which then falls to earth in rain.

Water Cycle

34

©2000 The Education Center, Inc. • Investigating Science • Plants • TEC1733 • Key p. 48

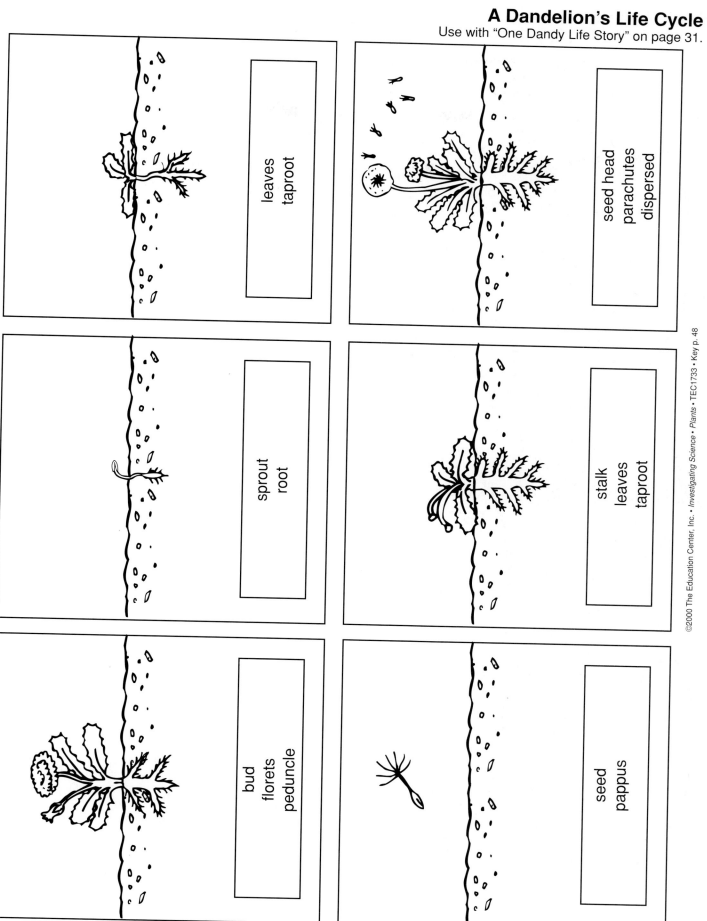

leaves
taproot

seed head
parachutes
dispersed

sprout
root

stalk
leaves
taproot

bud
florets
peduncle

seed
pappus

©2000 The Education Center, Inc. • Investigating Science • Plants • TEC1733 • Key p. 48

A Successful Succession of New Life

Fires, floods, mud slides, and other naturally occurring events can greatly affect a forest's plant and animal life. But are the effects all negative? *Succession* is a term used to describe a type of natural regrowth that occurs in an area that has been visited by one of these events. Follow the directions below to discover one forest's story.

Directions:
1. Read the paragraph in each box below. Use the words from the bank to fill in the blanks.
2. Cut out the five boxes and place them in the correct order of succession.
3. Cut three 9" x 12" sheets of construction paper in half. Glue each box to the center of a different half. Illustrate the stage of succession around the box.
4. On the remaining half sheet, design a decorative cover including a title and your name.
5. Use a hole puncher to make two holes about half an inch from the bottom edge of the cover. Do the same to the top of the last sheet. Then punch two holes along the tops and bottoms of the remaining four sheets, making sure all of the holes are aligned.
6. Finally, use yarn or string to tie the six sheets together to make one long strip.

Word Bank

sunlight	seeds	years	walnut
burrowed	wildflowers	branches	grow
aspens	Douglas	plants	shelter
decay	natural	ground	minerals

The Intermediate Forest Stage
Small trees grew taller, especially pines and (1)_____. (After about 20 years they became about 40 feet tall.) These trees provided homes and (2)_____ for animals such as owls, chipmunks, squirrels, foxes, and woodpeckers. The newer plants that once covered the ground died due to these trees blocking the (3)_____.

The Thicket Stage
The (1)_____ from the previous stage continued dying. Perennials, dense shrubs, and thorny vines covered the (2)_____. With this new ground cover, animals such as rabbits, snakes, and skunks returned. After about ten years, trees began to (3)_____ .

The Fire Stage
Most animals, such as bears and elk, were able to outrun the fire and survived. Other animals, such as squirrels and mice, (1)_____ underground and were not harmed. The fire cleared away most of the dead logs, leaves, and other debris from the florest floor. Some trees, such as the (2)_____ fir and ponderosa pine, were able to resist the fire and remain standing while some pine trees used the fire to help their cones burst open and scatter their (3)_____. The ground became covered with ash that is rich in calcium, phosphorus, and other (4)_____. Insects, birds, and some small animals returned right away to forage for seeds or other small animals.

The Mature Forest Stage
Pines and aspens were replaced by *deciduous* trees, such as oak, hickory, sycamore, and (1)_____. Many animals such as skunks, salamanders, insects, snakes, and birds began thriving, finding food and shelter in dead trees and fallen (2)_____. Mosses and mushrooms grew. The forest reached its last stage and remained for many years. Another (3)_____ or man-made event may cause this process to begin again.

The Meadow Stage
Annuals, such as herbs, grasses, horseweed, and (1)_____ began to grow from undamaged roots and scattered seeds. Insects, spiders, snails, worms, and birds returned. This stage lasted about five (2)_____, and then the plants began to die and (3)_____. Valuable nutrients then returned to the soil, helping the next stage of plants to grow.

Note to the teacher: Provide students with scissors, glue, three 9" x 12" sheets of light-colored construction paper, yarn or string, access to a hole puncher, and crayons or markers. For a sample showing construction of the project, see "Take a Stand!" on page 33.

Name _____

Problem solving

Life Cycle Lingo

Follow the directions below to find the missing life cycle vocabulary words.

Directions: Read each definition. Write a letter from the grid that matches each ordered pair of symbols below the definition. Hint: To find each letter, read the grid across and then up.

1. the process of a new plant growing from part of an existing plant

   ___ ___ ___ ___ ___ ___ ___ ___ ___ ___ ___

2. absorbed through a plant's leaves to make carbohydrates

   ___ ___ ___ ___ ___ ___ ___ ___ ___ ___ ___ ___ ___

3. develop in the flowering parts of plants and begin the next life cycle

   ___ ___ ___ ___ ___

4. used by plants to make protein

   ___ ___ ___ ___ ___ ___ ___ ___

5. when a plant or plant community reaches full growth

   ___ ___ ___ ___ ___ ___ ___ ___

6. the sprouting or growth of a seed

   ___ ___ ___ ___ ___ ___ ___ ___ ___ ___ ___

7. brought through the soil by water to help plants grow

   ___ ___ ___ ___ ___ ___ ___ ___ ___

8. the natural replacing of one plant community for another

   ___ ___ ___ ___ ___ ___ ___ ___ ___ ___

9. the spreading or scattering of seeds

   ___ ___ ___ ___ ___ ___ ___ ___ ___

10. to rot or decay

   ___ ___ ___ ___ ___ ___ ___ ___ ___

	A	B	C	D	E
(tree)	F	G	H	I	J
(flower)	K	L	M	N	O
(grass)	P	Q	R	S	T
(drop)	U	V	W	X	Y

(leaf) (tree) (flower) (grass) (drop)

Trees

What can grow higher than a 30-story building and live thousands of years? A tree! Use this collection of activities to introduce your students to this fascinating and important natural resource.

Leif Nutley's Arboretum

Scotch Pine
Cone-shaped evergreen tree. It has needles for leaves. This tree doesn't have fruit. The seeds are found inside cones.

Otter Creek

Lost Lake

Busy Beaver Cove

A Walk in the Park
(Research, Critical Thinking, Art)

The path to learning about deciduous and evergreen trees starts with students planning and mapping their own arboretums. Begin by explaining that *evergreen* trees stay green all year, replacing their old leaves or needles for new ones a few at a time. *Deciduous* trees lose their leaves at the same time each year. The green-colored chlorophyll in deciduous trees breaks down in the autumn. Then the bright, hidden colors of leaves appear before they fall off.

To learn more about these types of trees, divide your class into small groups. Provide field guides and other reference materials that describe both kinds of trees. Give each group a large sheet of poster board and have students work together to design an arboretum featuring a path winding through a collection of both tree types. Have each group include at least three different trees from each main group. Instruct groups to sketch, color, and then label the trees, creating a pleasant and informative map for visitors. Tell them to include each tree's name on the label, along with a description of its shape, leaves, and fruit. Encourage students to add birds and animals in appropriate places. (For example, a robin might be shown eating chokecherry fruit, or a beaver might be shown near an aspen or willow.) When the maps are complete, have each group present its nature center guide to the class.

Background for the Teacher

- The three main parts of a tree are the *trunk* and *branches,* the *leaves,* and the *roots.* The branches and leaves together form the *crown.*
- The two main groups of trees are *needleleaf* and *broadleaf.* Most needleleaf trees produce cones and are called *conifers.* Most broadleaf trees lose their leaves in the autumn and are described as *deciduous.*
- Broadleaf trees may have *simple* (single leaf attached to one stalk) or *compound* (separate leaves attached to one stalk) leaves. *Double compound* leaves are further divided into still smaller leaflets.
- The edges of broadleaf trees may be *smooth, lobed,* or *toothed.* The vein patterns in leaves of different trees vary as well.
- The trunks, branches, and roots of broadleaf and needleleaf trees are made of four layers of tissue. Arranged from the innermost layer out, they are the *xylem, cambium, phloem,* and *cork.*
- The *xylem* (the woody, central part of the trunk), carries water and dissolved minerals from the roots to the leaves where chloroplasts use the water to make food sugar. The *phloem* carries food made in the leaves to other tree parts.

A Forest of Tree Books

A Tree Is Growing by Arthur Dorros (Scholastic Inc., 1997)

The Giving Tree by Shel Silverstein (HarperCollins Juvenile Books, 1986)

The Lorax by Theodore Seuss Geisel (Dr. Seuss) (Random House, 1971)

My Favorite Tree: Terrific Trees of North America by Diane Iverson (Dawn Publications, 1999)

Sky Tree: Seeing Science Through Art by Thomas Locker (HarperCollins Publishers, Inc.; 1995)

Tree (Eyewitness Books) by David Burnie (Alfred A. Knopf, Inc.; 1988)

Tree Sensations
(Investigation, Descriptive Writing)

This multisensory activity will encourage students to appreciate trees in new ways. Ahead of time, find several trees on your school grounds that student groups can safely observe. (Make sure each tree is free from poisonous vines, stinging insects, etc.) Give each student five 5" x 8" index cards, scissors, and a copy of the directions below. With one card, have the student create a viewing frame by cutting a 2" x 3" window in it. Instruct each student to label the remaining cards "sight," "hearing," "smell," and "touch." Next, divide the class into small groups, assigning one schoolyard tree to each group. Then have the groups complete the activities below and record their observations on their notecards. Once back inside the classroom, have students visit one another's trees by viewing their classmates' cards through their notecard frames.

Touch

Hearing
singing
fluttering
chirping
swishing
scratching

Directions for each group:

1. Lie on your back under the tree and look up at its *crown* (leaves and branches) through the index card frame. Focus on the details of the branches and leaves. On the notecard labeled "sight," sketch the crown and write five nouns that name the details you observe.
2. Continue to lie on the ground, but close your eyes. Listen for sounds coming from the tree. List five verbs that tell what you hear on the "hearing" notecard.
3. Stand near the tree. Touch any of the tree's roots, trunk, branches, and leaves that you can reach. On the notecard labeled "touch," name each tree part and describe the way it feels to you.
4. Close your eyes again. Sniff the trunk, leaves, buds, and any other parts of the tree you can reach. On the "smell" notecard, list words that describe odors you notice.

Trees Over Time
(Journaling/Art)

Help students become increasingly aware of subtle growth, seasonal changes, and the simple beauty of trees with this unique journaling activity. Begin by sharing the book *Sky Tree: Seeing Science Through Art* by Thomas Locker (see publishing information on page 38) with your class. Guide students to identify the tree's changes captured by the author and artist. Then have each student select a tree near her home to study. Have her write about it regularly over a predetermined period of time. To make each journal unique, have each student choose to include the activities from the following list.

Journal Activities:
- Photograph your tree once a week. Mount the photographs in your journal. Write a few sentences to describe how the tree changed.
- Draw the tree as it looks now. Then draw the tree the way you think it will look six months from now.
- Write a poem describing your tree as a home for wild creatures. Include details about the living things that share the tree home.
- Look closely at the tree's size, shape, bark, and leaves. Then draw illustrations of the tree and its leaves, buds, flowers, fruit, and seeds.

Guide to Leaf Collecting
(Exploration, Art)

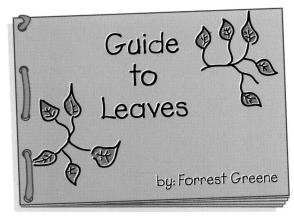

Use this variation on the standard leaf collection to help your amateur naturalists focus on leaf characteristics that will help them identify trees. Ahead of time, make a class supply of the chart shown at the bottom of page 43. Point out the various leaf edges and vein patterns while explaining *simple, compound,* and *double compound* leaf structures (see the background information on page 38). Allow students time to collect examples of each leaf type, referring to the chart as they search. Direct students to store collected leaves between paper towels pressed under several heavy books.

Point out that some leaf variations (such as the parallel veins in ginkgo leaves) may not grow naturally in your area. Have students use reference books to find and draw illustrations of these leaves to complete their collections. Then guide students through the steps below to organize their leaf collections into attractive reference guides.

Materials for each student: four 9" x 12" sheets of construction paper, four 9" x 12" sheets of clear Con-Tact® paper, double-sided transparent tape, 12" length of raffia, access to a hole puncher

Steps:

1. Create an attractive title page for the collection on one construction paper sheet.
2. Label the three remaining pages as follows: "Leaf Edges," "Vein Patterns," and "Leaflet Variations."
3. Sort the pressed leaves by group and then lay them out on the pages.
4. Using double-sided tape, position the pressed leaves (or leaf illustrations) on the pages. Label each leaf with the featured characteristic and the name of the tree (if known).
5. Carefully cover each page with Con-Tact paper.
6. Punch a series of holes along the left side of the pages. Then use raffia to bind the pages together.

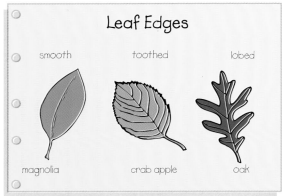

A Medley of Leaf Prints
(Art)

Leaf printing is a fun, creative way for your budding botanists to preserve the beauty and characteristics of leaves they have collected. Ahead of time, have each student bring in five or six *simple* (single leaf attached to one stalk) leaves from one tree. Then set up five different centers for each stage of the leaf-printing activity. Make five copies of page 44 and gather the supplies listed on that page for each center. Cover the work surfaces at each center with newspaper and then display the supplies along with a copy of page 44 in each center.

Divide students into five groups and assign a starting center for each group. Review the directions on page 44 for making each type of leaf print and the frame. Then circulate groups of students through the centers. As students finish their prints, have them lay their prints on their desks to dry. When the frames are finished and the leaf prints are dry, have each student securely tape his prints facedown on the back of his frame. Display the prints in your classroom. Then invite your students to take them home to share with their families.

How Tall Is That Tree, Anyway?
(Math, Writing)

Convince your students that they can measure the height of a tree without even climbing it! Pair students and provide each pair with a pencil, a Popsicle® stick, and a yardstick. Take students outdoors. Have each pair estimate the height of a chosen tree and record its estimate. Then direct each pair to measure its tree as follows.

Have Student A hold the Popsicle stick and Student B hold the pencil. Direct Student B to extend his arm, holding the pencil vertically out in front of him. Then have him back away from the tree, stopping when the pencil and tree appear to be the same height. Next, have Student B turn the pencil horizontally, lining up the pencil point with the base of the tree trunk.

Instruct Student A to move away from the tree until it appears to Student B that his partner is standing even with the eraser of the pencil. Have Student A push the Popsicle stick into the ground to mark the distance. Finally, have the student pair use the yardstick to measure the distance from the base of the tree to the Popsicle stick. The measurement should equal the approximate height of the tree. Have the student pair record the height.

Upon returning to the classroom, have the students find the difference between their original estimates and their tree's measurements. Discuss possible reasons why people might want to know the height of a tree. If desired, spark ideas for a writing assignment with a story starter like the one shown at the left.

What a Story!
A hurricane was approaching the city where Mark lived. Mark knew that his father was worried that the big old pine tree could fall during the storm. The family's new garage was only 50 feet away from the base of the tree. Would the old pine tree hit the garage if it fell in that direction?

Deciduous Trees Freeze Tag
(Game)

In this exciting variation on the outdoor game of freeze tag, students representing deciduous trees lose their leaves and freeze at Jack Frost's chilly touch. (Fortunately, evergreen tree players are ever-ready to help their deciduous friends!)

Ahead of time, cut out a supply of deciduous leaf and evergreen tree shapes in two different colors. Then divide students into two teams. Assign each team a color and distribute an equal number of tree and leaf shapes in that color to team members. Have each team member, except one, tape one shape to his shirt. Appoint the one remaining student from each team to play the role of Jack Frost and give both of these students a hat to wear. Place a basket containing 15 extra leaves of both colors and tape at the edge of the playing field. Then explain the directions and let the play begin!

Directions:
1. At a starting signal, each Jack Frost chases the students on the opposite team who are wearing deciduous leaves.
2. When tagged, a deciduous player freezes and gives Jack Frost his leaf.
3. An evergreen player can unfreeze a teammate by replacing the teammate's leaf with one (of the same color) from the basket. Players cannot take more than one leaf at a time from the basket.
4. The game is over when all of the deciduous players on a team are frozen and no leaves in that team's colors remain in the basket.

Collage of Tree Treasures
(Critical Thinking, Art)

Trees provide more than shade and colorful autumn scenery. Help your students recognize the value of trees with this informative collage. Ahead of time, cut out a large trunk shape from brown paper. Also, cut out a tree crown from green paper. Tape the tree pieces onto a wall, adding the title "Giving Trees." Then read aloud *The Giving Tree* by Shel Silverstein (see publishing information on page 38). Discuss the gifts the tree provided to the boy in the story. Guide students to conclude that trees enrich people's lives in many ways. Then have your students brainstorm a list of valuable tree products—such as wood, paper, and fruit—and list them on the chalkboard. Challenge students to include on the list unusual products such as cork, cinnamon, coffee, and rubber. Next, direct students to leaf through magazines and catalogs and cut out pictures of tree products. Have the students glue the pictures onto the paper tree. Encourage students to continue adding pictures to the collage as the study of trees leads them to discover new reasons to appreciate these special giving trees.

The Positive (and Negative) Side of Conservation
(Literature, Critical Thinking, Art)

Spark interest in tree resource management with this literature-based activity. Ahead of time, obtain copies of *The Lorax* by Dr. Seuss (see publishing information on page 38) and *The Truax* by Terri Birkett (see ordering suggestions below). Read and discuss both books, pointing out that each one expresses exaggerated views of an important issue—tree resource management. Use the questions shown in the boxes to stimulate discussion and to help students identify and understand the issue. Note negative and positive management practices on the chalkboard as they are mentioned during the discussion. *(For example, a negative practice might include cutting trees, which would disturb wildlife homes. A positive practice might include cutting trees to allow new species to move into areas that previously did not have sufficient sunlight.)*

Then pair students and give each pair two 9" x 12" sheets of construction paper: one green and one gray. Have students cut the green sheet in half, making one half look like a battery, and then glue the halves to opposite ends of the gray paper. On one end of the green paper, have the pair describe an activity that has a negative effect on the environment. On the other end, have the pair describe a positive alternative that benefits the environment. Then have the students illustrate the positive alternative on the battery's gray center. Display the batteries on a bulletin board with the title "Trees Energize the Environment."

Trees Energize the Environment

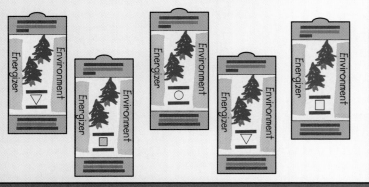

Discussion Questions:
The Lorax
- What was the Truffula forest like before the Once-ler began cutting down trees?
- What wild creatures depended on the Truffula Trees?
- What products did the Once-ler make out of the Truffula tree tufts?

The Truax
- Why didn't the Guardbark want trees cut down?
- What products were made from the trees cut by Truax?
- What did Truax do to protect trees as a resource?

To order copies of *The Truax*:
Write (on school letterhead stationery) to the National Oak Flooring Manufacturers Association, P. O. Box 3009, Memphis, TN 38173-0009 to request free copies of *The Truax*. This book was funded by the Hardwood Forest Foundation and the National Oak Flooring Manufacturers Association. *The Truax* is also available online at: http://www.nofma.org/truax.htm (as of July 2000).

Town Meeting
(Research, Simulation)

This motivating town meeting simulation will give students an opportunity to learn more about forest management issues. Begin by explaining that local interest groups often attempt to persuade decision makers (government officials) to use available land in certain ways. Then divide the students into six groups—five special interest groups and one group of town officials. Tell students to pretend that their town has just been given 150 acres of forestland and that they will decide how it will be used. Give each group a description from the list shown. Have each group use reference books to help prepare a case supporting its interest. Each group's case should include five positive effects its plan will have on the community and the environment. Direct the town officials to develop a list of questions for each of the special interest groups, such as "Will any animal habitats be destroyed?" and "How many old trees will you cut down?"

Next, set up the room to resemble a town meeting with the officials in the front of the classroom. Have the groups take turns presenting their cases to the officials and answering their questions. Have the officials summarize each presentation and record the group's most valid points on the chalkboard. When all the cases have been presented, allow time for the class to consider the merits of each case and vote for one land-use proposal.

Citizens for Forests: An environmental group determined to protect forests from any kind of development.
Lumber for Luxury: A group interested in supplying wood products to furniture, flooring, and paneling companies.
Humans for Houses: A group of builders interested in providing nice, affordable apartments for poorer people.
Committee for Business Growth: A group interested in clearing land to bring large companies and shopping centers to the community to build the local economy.
Parents for Recreation: A group of parents interested in building playgrounds, soccer fields, public pools, hiking trails, and other recreational facilities for children.

Chart
Use with "A Guide to Leaf Collecting" on page 40.

Number of blades	Leaf edges	Vein patterns

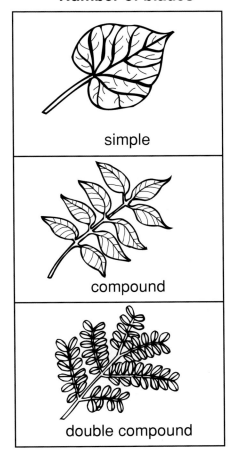

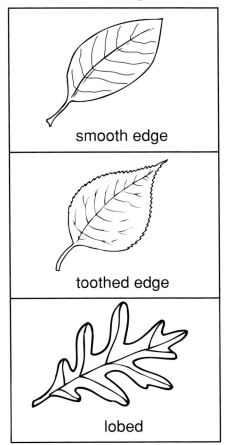

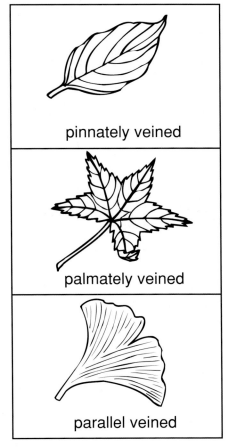

Leaf Medley Art Project

Center 1: Leaf Stamp Print
Materials for each student: leaf, quarter sheet of white copy paper, waxed paper, scrap paper, stamp pad

1. Lay the veined side of the leaf on the stamp pad. Cover the leaf with waxed paper.
2. Rub the leaf through the waxed paper until the leaf is covered with ink.
3. Carefully pick up the leaf and discard the waxed paper.
4. Lay the inked side of the leaf in the center of the white paper.
5. Cover it with scrap paper. Being careful not to let the leaf move, rub it lightly to transfer the ink to the white paper.
6. Discard the leaf and scrap paper. Lay the print on your desk to dry.

Center 2: Leaf Pencil Drawing
Materials for each student: leaf, quarter sheet of white copy paper, soft-lead drawing pencils

1. Lay the leaf in the center of the white paper sheet and trace around the edges.
2. Study the leaf's vein patterns and draw them onto the resulting paper leaf. Discard the leaf.
3. Shade the paper leaf, using a variety of light and dark pencil tones.

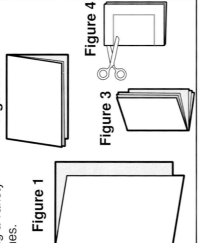

Figure 1

Figure 2

Figure 3

Figure 4

Center 3: Sponge-Painted Leaf Stencil
Materials for each student: leaf, 6" square of tagboard, quarter sheet of white copy paper, scissors, small soft sponge, poster paints (in fall colors) in shallow dishes, paper towels

1. Place the leaf on the tagboard and trace its outline.
2. Cut along the outline of the leaf to form your stencil.
3. Dip the sponge lightly into the paint. Gently dab excess paint on paper towels.
4. Holding the leaf stencil firmly on the paper, gently dab the sponge on the open-leaf stencil, using a straight up and down tapping motion.
5. Give the stencil an autumn look by repeating the process with several colors of paint.
6. Carefully lift the tagboard to avoid smearing the paint. Lay the stenciled leaf on your desk to dry.

Center 5: Project Frame
Materials for each student: one 9" x 12" sheet of construction paper, ruler, scissors

1. Hold the construction paper horizontally and make the following folds: fold it in half from left to right (Figure 1); fold it in half from top to bottom (Figure 2); fold it in half again from left to right (Figure 3).
2. Leaving it folded, draw a half-inch border along the top, right, and bottom sides.
3. Cut out a window along the border lines (Figure 4).
4. Unfold the paper to reveal four windows.

Center 4: Leaf Sun Print
Materials for each student: leaf, 6" square of Sunprint® paper, 8" square of stiff cardboard, double-sided transparent tape, quart-sized food-storage bag, water in a shallow pan

1. Tape the leaf in the center of the Sunprint paper with the more heavily veined side down.
2. Tape the Sunprint paper and leaf to the cardboard and slip them into the bag.
3. Set the leaf in direct sunlight and leave it undisturbed. After three to ten minutes, carefully peek under the corner of the leaf to see that the color of the Sunprint paper has changed.
4. Take the layers apart. Discard the leaf. Rinse the Sunprint paper in the pan of water for one minute.
5. Lay the print on your desk to dry.

Note to the teacher: Use with "A Medley of Leaf Prints" on page 40. Sunprint paper can be purchased from educational supply companies.

44

"TREE-mendous" Projects

Climb the tree of knowledge with these fun tree-themed activities. Color the leaf after completing each activity.

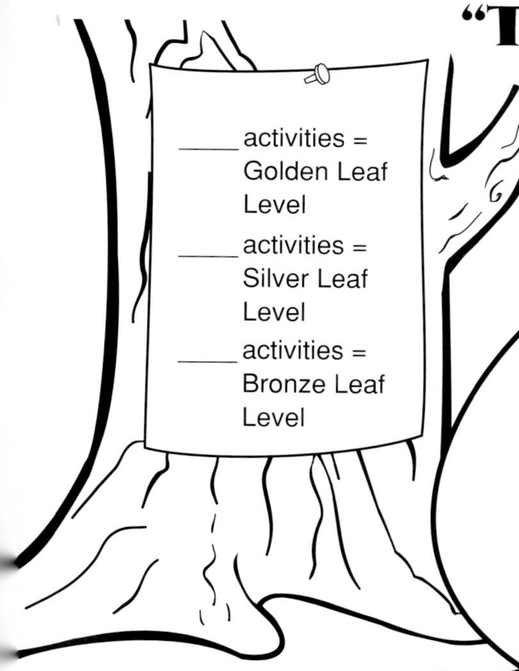

_____ activities =
Golden Leaf
Level

_____ activities =
Silver Leaf
Level

_____ activities =
Bronze Leaf
Level

"Poe-tree"
Look through poetry books to find a poem about trees. Carefully copy the poem onto a sheet of paper and identify its author. Illustrate the poem. Then, on the back of the sheet, tell how the author used scientific facts about trees in the poem.

Tree Game
Design a game about trees and their products. Make a gameboard, question cards, or leaf identification cards to accompany your game. Include directions and rules for playing. Be sure to base the game on facts about trees.

Arbor Day
Write a paragraph about Arbor Day. Tell who suggested it and where and when it was first celebrated. Explain what you think Arbor Day's founder meant when he said that this holiday is different from others because it celebrates the future instead of the past.

Tree Detectives
Write a set of clues about three schoolyard trees that will lead your classmates to identify each one. Give hints about the shape, leaves, flowers, and seeds of each tree.

Tree-Friendly Tree House
Design and draw the ultimate tree house! Describe the kind of tree you would choose as the ideal location for your tree house. Make a list of the materials you would need to build the structure. Then cross out all of the wood products on your list and suggest materials other than wood to use in building your tree-friendly tree house.

John Chapman
Write a short biography of John Chapman. Include answers to these questions: What is his more famous nickname? In what states did he live and travel? How did he turn his love of nature into the important work for which he became famous?

Tree Book Review
Make a bibliography listing five of your favorite books about trees. After listing the information for each book, write a brief review describing the book and telling why you like it.

©2000 The Education Center, Inc. • *Investigating Science • Plants* • TEC1733

Note to the teacher: Program a copy of the contract and choose a reward, such as a special treat or privilege, for each level of completion. Then make a copy of the contract for each student. Have the student select the number of activities she will complete. After the student meets her goal, treat her with the designated reward.

Name_____

A Slice of Tree Life

A close look at a cross section or slice of a tree trunk can tell you a lot about the age and growing conditions of the tree.

Directions: Study the tree slices shown below to answer the questions that follow. Use reference materials for help, if needed.

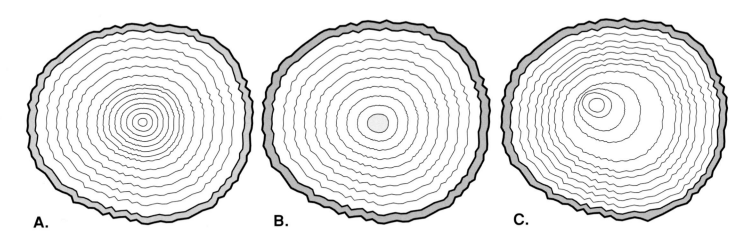

A.   B.   C.

1. Fast spring and early summer growth appears as _____-colored rings.

2. Late summer and early fall growth is slower and appears as _____-colored rings.

3. Counting the ring pairs is a way to estimate the _____ of the tree when it was cut.

4. Approximately how old is each of the trees shown? A. _____ B. _____ C. _____

5. Explain how it is possible for the trees shown to be different ages but have the same *diameter* (distance across the slice). _____

_____

6. Which tree may have grown in a place where it was exposed to the wind? *(Hint: The tree grew faster on the side facing away from the wind.)* _____

7. Trees need sunlight and water to grow. Which tree may have experienced a drought after about five years? _____

8. Which tree may have begun to get more sunlight and water after its neighbor fell down? _____

9. Which tree grew at the steadiest rate? _____

Bonus Box: Draw a tree slice on the back of this paper. Then write a paragraph about the tree's age and possible growing conditions.

 ©2000 The Education Center, Inc. • *Investigating Science • Plants* • TEC1733 • Key p. 48

Distinguishing Deciduous Trees

Directions: Use reference materials to find out more about the deciduous trees listed below. Match each tree to its leaf and seed. Then choose a term from the list that describes each leaf. (Some leaf terms may be used more than once.) Write your answers in the provided blanks.

Trees: White Oak   Fremont Cottonwood   Sweet Gum
American Sycamore   Black Cherry   Ginkgo
Sugar Maple   Black Walnut   Paper Birch   Honeylocust

Leaf Terms: simple leaf   compound leaf   pinnate veins
palmate veins   parallel veins   toothed edge   lobed edge
smooth edge

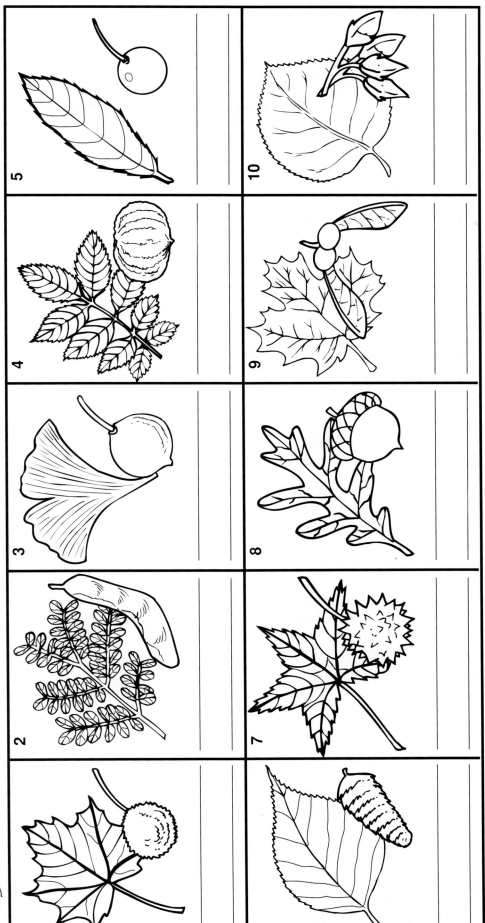

©2000 The Education Center, Inc. • *Investigating Science • Plants • TEC1733* • Key p. 48

Answer Keys

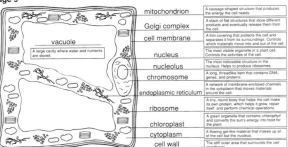

Page 9

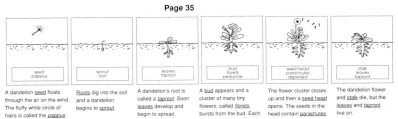

mitochondrion	A sausage-shaped structure that produces the energy the cell needs.
Golgi complex	A stack of flat structures that store different products and eventually release them from the cell.
cell membrane	A thin covering that protects the cell and separates it from its surroundings. Controls which materials move into and out of the cell.
nucleus	The most visible organelle in a plant cell. Controls the activities of the cell.
nucleolus	The most noticeable structure in the nucleus. Helps to produce ribosomes.
chromosome	A long, threadlike item that contains DNA, genes, and proteins.
endoplasmic reticulum	A network of membrane-enclosed channels in the cytoplasm that moves materials around the cell.
ribosome	A tiny, round body that helps the cell make its own protein, which helps it grow, repair itself, and perform chemical operations.
chloroplast	A green organelle that contains *chlorophyll* and converts the sun's energy into food for the plant.
cytoplasm	A flowing gel-like material that makes up all of the cell but the *nucleus*.
cell wall	The stiff outer area that surrounds the *cell membrane*.

vacuole — A large cavity where water and nutrients are stored.

Page 10

Students' answers may be glued in any order.
Roots: carrot, radish, sweet potato
Bulbs: onion, garlic
Stems: asparagus, green onion, celery stalk
Leaves: cabbage, lettuce, spinach
Flowers: broccoli floret, cauliflower
Fruits: apple, cucumber, pumpkin, tomatoes, pepper
Seeds: peas, beans, corn, peanut

Page 11

1. poison ivy
2. jack-in-the-pulpit
3. belladonna
4. ragweed
5. oleander
6. rhubarb
7. mushroom
8. dogbane
9. hemlock

Coded answer: Never eat or chew a plant you don't know well.

Page 21
Part One:
1. sun; transpiration; evaporates
2. stomata
3. absorbs; cool
4. roots; water
5. stem; xylem vessels
Part Two:
1. perspiration
2. pores
3. meat, cheese, and bread
4. arteries and veins
5. vitamins and minerals
Bonus Box answer: Students' analogies will vary.

Page 22

Students' explanations will vary but should mention that humans get their oxygen from plants during photosynthesis. Students should also mention that plants get the carbon dioxide they need to make food from the air that humans breathe out during respiration.
Bonus Box answer: *Anaerobic* means respiration without air. Students' sentences will vary.

Page 23
1. air
2. soil
3. light
4. light and air
5. water
6. water and air
7. soil
8. light and air
9. soil
10. water

Page 27
Monocot
Seed one *cotyledon*, or seed "leaf"
Root similarly sized, branching roots
Stem usually *herbaceous* (nonwoody) stems with scattered *vascular bundles* (tubes through which sap travels)
Leaf narrow leaves with parallel veins
Flower petals are in threes; *sepals* (leaflike structures below the flower) and petals are hard to tell apart
Examples iris, grass, lily, palm tree, corn
Dicot
Seed two *cotyledons*, or seed "leaves"
Root one main root *(taproot)* with very small roots branching off of it
Stem both woody and *herbaceous* (nonwoody) stems with *vascular bundles* (tubes through which sap travels) in rings
Leaf broad leaves with branching veins
Flower petals are in fours or fives; petals and *sepals* (leaflike structures below the flower) are easy to tell apart
Examples peanut, bean, violet, maple tree

Page 28
1. 15 days
2. March 18
3. 2 to 2½ feet
4. *Leucantheum maximum 'Alaska'*
5. Yes, it's a perennial.
6. Full sun or partial shade
7. May
8. February
9. Enough to keep the soil fairly moist
10. Harvesting the flowers
11. 3–4 inches
12. False. They should be sown ⅛ inch deep.

Page 29

The vegetable garden shown is only one possible variation of how students can use their allotted space. There should, however, be some similarities. Corn, beans, and tomatoes are tall vegetables and should be in the back of the garden or on the side, unless you need to use them to give other vegetables partial shade. The carrots need morning sun, so they should probably be on the right side. However, if there are no beans, corn, or tomatoes planted to their right (so they're still receiving morning sun), then they can be elsewhere. The green onions and the lettuce grow best in partial sun. There should be some shade on these vegetables at some time during the day.

N
W E
S

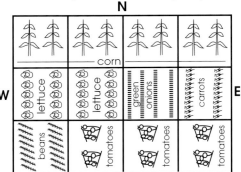

Green Onions
Sections Planted*
Number of Rows 4
Plants in Each Row 35
Lettuce
Sections Planted*
Number of Rows 2
Plants in Each Row 5
Carrots
Sections Planted*
Number of Rows 2
Plants in Each Row 11

Beans
Sections Planted*
Number of Rows 2
Plants in Each Row 8
Tomatoes
Sections Planted*
Number of Rows 1
Plants in Each Row 2
Corn
Sections Planted*
Number of Rows 1
Plants in Each Row 2

*Answers may vary.

Page 34

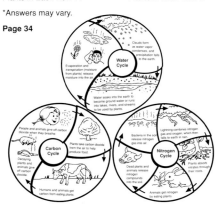

Page 35

seed pappus	sprout root	leaves taproot	bud florets peduncle	seed head parachutes dispersed	stalk leaves taproot

A dandelion *seed* floats through the air on the wind. The fluffy white circle of hairs is called the *pappus*.

Roots dig into the soil and a dandelion begins to *sprout*.

A dandelion's root is called a *taproot*. Soon *leaves* develop and begin to spread.

A *bud* appears and a cluster of many tiny flowers, called *florets*, bursts from the bud. Each flower cluster is held up by a stalk called a *peduncle*.

The flower cluster closes up and then a *seed head* opens. The seeds in the head contain *parachutes* that are *dispersed* by the wind.

The dandelion flower and *stalk* die, but the *leaves* and *taproot* live on.

Page 36
The Fire Stage
1. burrowed
2. Douglas
3. seeds
4. minerals
The Meadow Stage
1. wildflowers
2. years
3. decay

The Thicket Stage
1. plants
2. ground
3. grow
The Intermediate Forest Stage
1. aspens
2. shelter
3. sunlight
The Mature Forest Stage
1. walnut
2. branches
3. natural

Page 37
1. propagation
2. carbon dioxide
3. seeds
4. nitrogen
5. maturity
6. germination
7. nutrients
8. succession
9. dispersal
10. decompose

Page 46
1. light
2. dark
3. age
4. A. 13 years old
   B. 9 years old
   C. 11 years old
5. Answers will vary. Accept any reasonable responses. Students should demonstrate understanding that various conditions affect the growth of trees. For example, one tree may receive more rain or sunlight than another, and therefore, show increased growth.
6. C 7. C 8. A 9. B

Page 47
Students' answers for the leaf terms may vary.
1. American Sycamore: simple leaf; palmate veins; toothed edge; lobed edge
2. Honeylocust: compound leaf; pinnate veins; smooth edge
3. Ginkgo: simple leaf; parallel veins; lobed edge
4. Black Walnut: compound leaf; pinnate veins; toothed edge
5. Black Cherry: simple leaf; pinnate veins; toothed edge
6. Paper Birch: simple leaf; pinnate veins; toothed edge
7. Sweet Gum: simple leaf; palmate veins; toothed edge
8. White Oak: simple leaf; palmate veins; lobed edge
9. Sugar Maple: simple leaf; palmate veins; toothed edge; lobed edge
10. Fremont cottonwood: simple leaf; pinnate veins; toothed edge